PRAI

"In a world where habits and behaviors are highly digitized, Fabio Pereira bridges the gap between the physical and the virtual, helping us understand why we should be more conscious in our online and offline decision making."

Maria Augusta Ribeiro – specialist in Netnography and Digital Behavior

"The book Digital Nudge brought a new perspective to my mind, which is to think about the diversity and inclusion of data, not just about teams."

Lisiane Lemos – technology specialist and Forbes Under 30

"Technology has the potential of changing our life for the better if we learn how to harness its power. Fabio has managed to connect a number of different perspectives and leave sufficient amount of critical questions for both technology developers as technology users. This book is a great start in becoming a more responsible human"

Val Yonchev

"The book presents a delightful and useful reading about the power of the digital age on human behavior. It is an excellent source of reflection and change. "

Teresa M. M. Maciel – UFPE's CTO

FABIO PEREIRA

DIGITAL NUDGE

The hidden forces behind the 35,000 decisions we make every day

Editora Caroli
caroli.org

Copidesque
Juliana Cury Rodrigues
Graphic design, layout and cover
Vanessa Lima
Proofreading
Laura Folgueira and Alyne Azuma
Print
Forma certa

Avenida Itajaí, 310 – Petrópolis
Porto Alegre, RS 90470-140, Brasil
www.caroli.org/editora
contato@caroli.org

Cataloging-in-Publication Data (CIP)
Angélica Ilacqua CRB-8/7057

Pereira, Fabio
Digital nudge: the hidden forces behind the 35,000 decisions we make every day / Fabio Pereira. – 1st ed.- São Paulo: Editora Caroli, 2019.
192 p.

1. Technology - Psychological aspects 2. Technological innovations - Psychological aspects 3. Digital media 4. Internet 5. Human behavior I. Título

19-2453 CDD 306.46

Index for Systematic Catalog:
1. Technology - Psychological aspects

ACKNOWLEDGMENTS

I want to thank everyone around the world who learned something about Digital Nudge through any of my words. They might have been heard as podcasts or public speaking, read on a book, social media or in blogs, or in any other channel where I share information about Digital Nudge, a subject that inspires me so much and about which I am extremely passionate. Thank you for every Instagram direct message, email, WhatsApp message and feedback on the book's first edition and other works. It was through these pointers that I managed to evolve and write this second edition you have in your hands now.

Special thanks to the mentors and the people who inspired me and helped me to write this book:

- Thank you, **Paulo Caroli**, for being my editor, mentor, and great friend. Thank you for encouraging me, guiding me, and pushing me when I needed.
- Thank you, **Flávia Ávila**, for being an inspiration as one of the pioneers on the subject of Behavioral Economics in Brazil and for your continuous and valuable help during my journey.

> Thank you, **Vinícius Teles**, for inspiring me in 2005, when I met you and you had written the first book about Agile in Brazil. You made me think: "One day, I want to be like Vinícius."
> Thank you, **Dan Ariely**, for broadening my vision during our conversations, which have guided me through the research and writing process of this book.

I also want to thank my family, who has always supported me on this learning journey. I am grateful to my brother **Paulo Neto**, who encouraged me to watch movies in English without subtitles since I was a child; what I have learned from this was fundamental to my career. Without it I would not have gotten here, I would not have gone to Australia and learned so much there. To my sister, **Amanda**, such a sweet person who has always been by my side, listening to me and supporting me in the most important moments of my life. To my mother, **Maria Ângela,** who always says I am the best author in the world—mothers are like that, right? To **Gerlindo**, for one of his 35,000 daily decisions having been becoming my father and guiding me through so many important decisions in my life. To my brother **Felipe**, for being one of my best friends and always being present in my life when I most needed it.

I want to thank my life partner **Helica**, who is in this book not only in the chapter about when we met digitally on Instagram, but also in every word and every page we wrote together. I appreciate each day she has been by my side as I wrote this book, supporting me and giving me the strength to believe in it.

SUMMARY

FOREWORD

Only an expert can guide you, the reader, on this important learning journey about digital consciousness. And that person is Fabio Pereira, one of the great experts in Brazil to help you strengthen your digital mind. I met Fabio through a mutual friend when my company was on an assignment with ThoughtWorks, the company Fabio was working for at the time. This friend was the link between our affinity and the activities we carried out. As soon as our connection was established, he contacted me and made himself available to help with the project we were developing, so it could be sped up and have a greater impact on people. So, in our first interaction, I immediately realized how focused Fabio is, and how this amazing professional is absolutely committed and trustful in what he does. Our relationship has grown closer, and this has once again shown me his concern and vigorous dedication to share with as many people as possible this all-important topic that makes every consumer today more aware, more empowered to make much better decisions, considering that today's world is digital and we interact much more intensively with product offers, content, and information in our everyday lives.

The truth is that today's society is experiencing one of the greatest changes a generation has ever had to face. Technological advances affect not only careers, businesses, and governments, but also the very meaning of humanity. We can talk about Artificial Intelligence, which will affect all areas; voice recognition, which is increasingly accurate in performing various tasks; facial recognition, which is already a reality in many countries and used as a safety device; and, finally, the deployment of the 5G internet, one hundred times faster than the current version.

But why am I talking about all this? Because we are facing a time when work as we know it is about to change forever. We live in an age when data has become the new oil, technology companies have become the most valuable ones in the world, and a career as a software developer has never seen such a high demand all over the world.

In addition to these transformations that are being brought about worldwide as a result of technological advances, we are witnessing the growth of Generation Z (people born after the year 2000), the first one that was born in the digital world and does not know how the world was like without the internet. Another important point: By the end of 2019, this generation will be the majority of the world's population, comprising 32% of people.

These people come with completely different safety concepts, habits, and choices than previous generations. So, we are experiencing a generation that will transform the consumer society. They will rewrite the way companies, organizations, and even jobs are established. In other words, technological advances are demanding from individuals, companies, society, and nations a change in the attitude of "how I behave in relation to what is around me."

Currently technology is ubiquitous. We need to have digital knowledge; we need to understand how transactions and the digital environment behave. According to the McKinsey Global Institute, the demand for activities involving basic physical and manual cognitive skills will be greatly reduced by 2030. In contrast, the demand for activities involving high-level cognitive skills, along with those concerning social and emotional abilities, and especially technological competences, will increase.

Thus, because of this tripod (technological advances, growth of Generation Z, and increasing demand for technological skills in the coming years), it is extremely necessary in today's world to develop digital awareness, an understanding of this new world that is a result of the technological evolution. All of this is mandatory for professionals, companies, states, and nations that want to remain competitive, modern, innovative, and active in today's world.

That's why I say: You will be transformed by this book. Using a straightforward language and a straight-to-the-point approach, the next few pages will lead you through a learning process that will change the way you see the world, the way you decide and will add a digital spice to everything you do!

Mauricio Benvenutti

Bestselling author of Incansáveis *[Tireless] and* Audaz *[Daring]*

and business partner at StartSe

WHAT IS THE DIGITAL AGE?

35,000

Yes, 35,000! This is the average number of decisions a human being makes every day (according to *UNCTV Science*'s "How Many Daily Decisions Do We Make?" article), with over 200 of them being about food. It means around one decision every two seconds. That is a lot of decisions. They are small, large, impactful, irrelevant, conscious, and unconscious. What to eat? What to wear? Which way to take to work? Which college exam or MBA to take? Whom to date?

We live in a world with an increasing amount of information. Some figures presented on the portal *FortuneLords* prove it:

- Every hour, 18,000 hours of videos are uploaded to YouTube. That is, to follow and watch all this content, we would have to multiply our time by 18,000.
- Five billion videos are watched on YouTube per day.
- Ten percent of all photos in the world were taken in the last 45 days.

Amongst the 35,000 decisions you make every day, have you ever wondered how many are digital decisions? Digital decisions are the ones we make using devices such as smartphones, tablets, computers, wearables, virtual reality devices, etc.—or those that digital devices often make for us.

WHEN THE PHYSICAL AND DIGITAL WORLDS MERGE

In 2007, I was still living in Brazil and decided to apply to work for ThoughtWorks, a leading global consultancy in technology and digital transformation. I did about ten interviews, all through Skype. I was hired to work at ThoughtWorks Australia. I packed up everything I had in three bags and moved to the other side of the world, the land of kangaroos, where I ended up living for eight years until 2016.

While in Sydney, I talked to my family and friends from Brazil almost every day, despite the 12 to 14-hour time difference—I joked I was in the future. I worked with teams assigned in Australia, China, India, and New Zealand, and we communicated every day via webcams.

I've been using Google Maps and Waze for years every time I want to go somewhere and don't know the route. Speaking of that, who still remembers routes after Waze and Google Maps? During the eight years I lived in Australia, I never owned a car, but could have access to them through an app on my phone called GoGet. When I needed a car, I opened the app, found the nearest car, got into it, used it, and then paid by the hour with my credit card. Other times, I'd get an Uber.

Here's another example of the digital world merging with the physical one: I met my girlfriend on Instagram. That's right, it wasn't in a bar, in a club, in a theater or on Tinder—it was on Instagram! I made a digital decision to send her a direct message and then, when the conversation evolved from Instagram to WhatsApp—a breakthrough in any digitally-initiated relationship—, we met in person and started dating.

I have become passionate about Buddhism and meditation in recent years and use two apps to meditate: Headspace and 1 Giant Mind. In addition, I have meditation playlists on Spotify and go to the Buddhist center from time to time to learn, connect with people, and evolve spiritually.

I wear a digital watch where I can see all my meetings for the day, how many steps I walk, and how much I exercise I get (it warns me when I am standing still and suggests that I move).

I realized I wasn't going to the gym as much as I had committed myself to. So I added reminders to my calendar, and ten minutes before the schedule, the watch tells me: "Gym in ten minutes." This way, I feel guilty if I don't go, as I'd already made a commitment to my "past self" that I would. And the "present self," however busy it may be, wants to think about the "future self," but it's hard, isn't it? We know we have to do something, but we procrastinate, we wait until later... However, I'm glad I found some things to help me, like the reminder. It has been working, but I need to admit that it's not bulletproof.

I have my digital watch, my calendar, my Waze, but there are people who go beyond their digital interactions and decisions. When I worked at ThoughtWorks, there were two cyborgs: Neil Harbisson and Moon Ribas. Cyborgs are people who have technological implants in their body; today, it is common to refer to that as "body hacking" or "biohacking."

#DigitalNudge

AMONGST THE 35,000 DECISIONS YOU MAKE EVERY DAY, HAVE YOU EVER WONDERED HOW MANY ARE DIGITAL DECISIONS?

Neil sees the world in black and white because he was born with achromatopsia, a genetic disorder also known as "color blindness". He decided to find a solution to this in technology. With an antenna-like device implanted in the back of his head, he is able to "understand the colors" around him by antenna-transmitted sounds that translate colors into distinct vibrations. He says he "listens to colors."

Moon is an artist who has an implant in her arm that vibrates every time an earthquake happens anywhere on Earth. She describes the experience as "two beating hearts, one being her own, and the other, the Earth's" and created a dance called "Waiting for Earthquakes." In it, Moon stands waiting for an earthquake to happen anywhere in the world and dances to the rhythm of the earthquake.

On August 2nd, 2017, I was in Santiago, Chile, working for a client who was going through what we call "digital transformation." That is, how to transform an entire business of 140,000 people using technology. In that same day, I woke up in the middle of the night with my bed shaking. I thought it was a dream, got a little disoriented and then went back to sleep.

I woke up at 7 a.m. and saw the following news on Google: "Earthquake in Santiago at 3:15 a.m." I was shocked because I had never experienced an earthquake in my life. After the shocking news, I kept thinking that the same earthquake at 3:15 a.m. had made Moon Ribas's arm vibrate, wherever she was in the world. All of this thanks to the fact that sensors measure earthquakes and that there is technology that connects tectonic plates in Chile to a person's arm in real time.

If she were in a place in a very different time zone from Chile, she would probably be dancing to the same frequency that woke me up in the middle of the night, while I thought my shaking bed was a dream.

It seems almost unnecessary to explain that our physical world is merging with the digital world. It happens through smartphones full of apps for everything, tablets, computers, sensors, wearables, virtual and augmented reality, autonomous cars that can drive without drivers, and even mirrors that talk to us.

While I am writing this book, there is technology to:

> Drive cars.
> Judge if defendants are guilty or innocent.
> Diagnose diseases.
> Correct essays.
> Invest in the stock market.
> Analyze crops.
> Recognize images better than humans.
> Identify human emotions.
> Conduct orchestras.[1]

I am extremely passionate about events. I attended one in Singapore, where the world was shown a smart mirror that integrated into your bank account. You can ask the mirror: "Alexa, what is my balance?", and the mirror responds and shows it to you. Alexa is a digital assistant created by Amazon who listens to what we say and

[1] This took place at the Lucca Philharmonic Orchestra in 2017. Available at: <www.nature.com/news/reboot-for-the-ai-revolution-1.22826>. Accessed on: May 4, 2019.

#DigitalNudge

A COMPUTER HAS EVEN TALKED TO ANOTHER COMPUTER WITHOUT HUMANS KNOWING WHAT THEY TALKED ABOUT!

performs tasks. In the 2017 CES (Consumer Electronic Show) in Las Vegas, assistants like her appeared on products such as refrigerators, robots, smartphones, speakers, dryers, washing machines, vacuum cleaners, Wi-Fi routers, cars, and more. Alexa is just an example of this kind of technology, but there are other, like Google Assistant, Apple's Siri, and Microsoft's Cortana.

In 2016, my nephew Pedro visited me and kept playing Pokémon GO, a game that influenced people around the world to walk 144 billion steps.[2] It works with augmented reality that stimulates movement outdoors.

Understanding how these new technologies impact our lives is part of what I do in this ever-changing world. I worked for ten years at ThoughtWorks, and, at the end of 2018, took on the challenge of leading a Digital Innovation area at Red Hat, where I also work with people, decisions and how the digital world affects our lives.

We are human, we make decisions based on what we feel and think more in the short term than in the long term. We have cognitive limitations in our brain, our attention is limited, and we think we are rational and make rational decisions, but we are irrational and unconscious—digitally unconscious.

---

[2] MULKERIN, Tim. *It's Official: The Pokémon Go Craze Has A Big Impact on Americans' Physical Activity. Business Insider*, Oct. 11, 2016. Available at: <https://www.businessinsider.com/pokemon-go-physical-effect-scientific-study-microsoft-stanford-2016-10>. Accessed on: May 15, 2019.

WE THINK WE ARE RATIONAL AND MAKE RATIONAL DECISIONS, BUT WE ARE IRRATIONAL AND UNCONSCIOUS—**DIGITALLY UNCONSCIOUS.**

#DigitalNudge

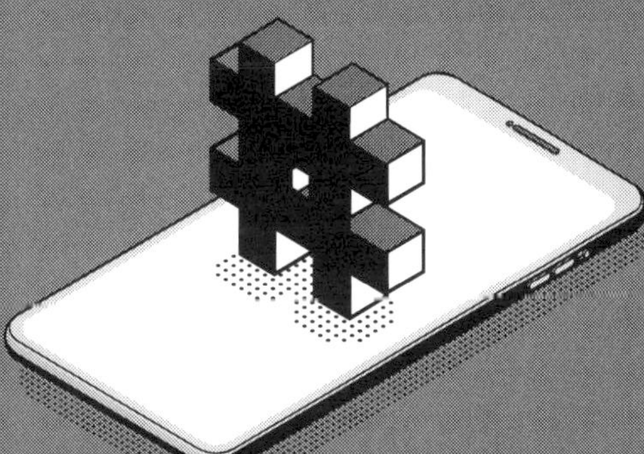

DIGITAL QUOTIENT (DQ): THE IQ AND EQ OF THE DIGITAL AGE

Sometimes we meet someone and think: "This person is not good at math but can communicate very well," or "This person doesn't speak well in public, but has a huge self-awareness of their emotions and behaviors." This happens because there is more than one type of intelligence. Howard Gardner explains it in his book *Structures of the Mind*, which described seven dimensions of intelligence. Since its publication in 1983, Gardner has proposed two new dimensions of intelligence: the naturalist and the existentialist. Today, this theory is known as the theory of multiple intelligences and is composed of nine intelligences:

1. Linguistics
2. Musical
3. Logical-mathematical
4. Visual/Spatial
5. Body/Kinesthetic
6. Interpersonal
7. Intrapersonal
8. Naturalist
9. Existentialist

The infographic below[3] shows the nine intelligences in a visual format:

[3] Based on: SOUZA, Taiz. *A Teoria das Inteligências Múltiplas de Gardner. Psiconlinews.com*, May 20, 2015. Available at: <https://psiconlinews.com/2015/05/teoria-das-inteligencias-multiplas-de-gardner.html >. Accessed in: May 4, 2019.

Source: ©Mark Vital. By Howard Gardner and Mark Vital. Available at: <https://blog.adioma.com/9-types-of-intelligence-infographic/>. Accessed on: October 10, 2019.

The popular Intelligence Quotient (IQ) only considers some of these intelligences, especially logical-mathematical, linguistic, and spatial. The Emotional Quotient (EQ) has brought a broader look at interpersonal and intrapersonal intelligences, showing that both are very important for a person's success and happiness. That is, EQ has made it clear that just having a high IQ is not enough.

As we said before, we already live in a world where computers drive cars, judge if defendants are guilty or innocent, diagnose diseases, correct essays, invest in the stock market, and much more. Will our current knowledge and today's teachings be needed in the future? The quick answer is: no! There are several other necessary and very important skills.

So, what is the answer? How to be sure if we already know what we need to know? How to learn? The Digital Intelligence Quotient (IQ), created by the DQ Institute, can be seen as a possible answer to this question. The DQ definition is continuously evolving; here's the September 2019 one, according to the DQ Institute:

> *Digital Intelligence (DQ) is a comprehensive set of technical, cognitive, meta-cognitive, and socio-emotional competencies that are grounded in universal moral values and that enable individuals to face the challenges and harness the opportunities of digital life. DQ has three levels, eight areas, and 24 competencies composed of knowledge, skills, attitudes, and values.*

In 2017, while I was working on the Portuguese version of this book, I approached the DQ Institute, and they allowed me to work on the first translation of the DQ Framework into Portuguese. The book was the first to release this content in Brazil. Now that it is being published in English, I still believe it's relevant to mention DQ as one of the main sources of a set of competencies and values that will allow us to live better lives in the digital age we are. So here is a summary of the DQ Framework:

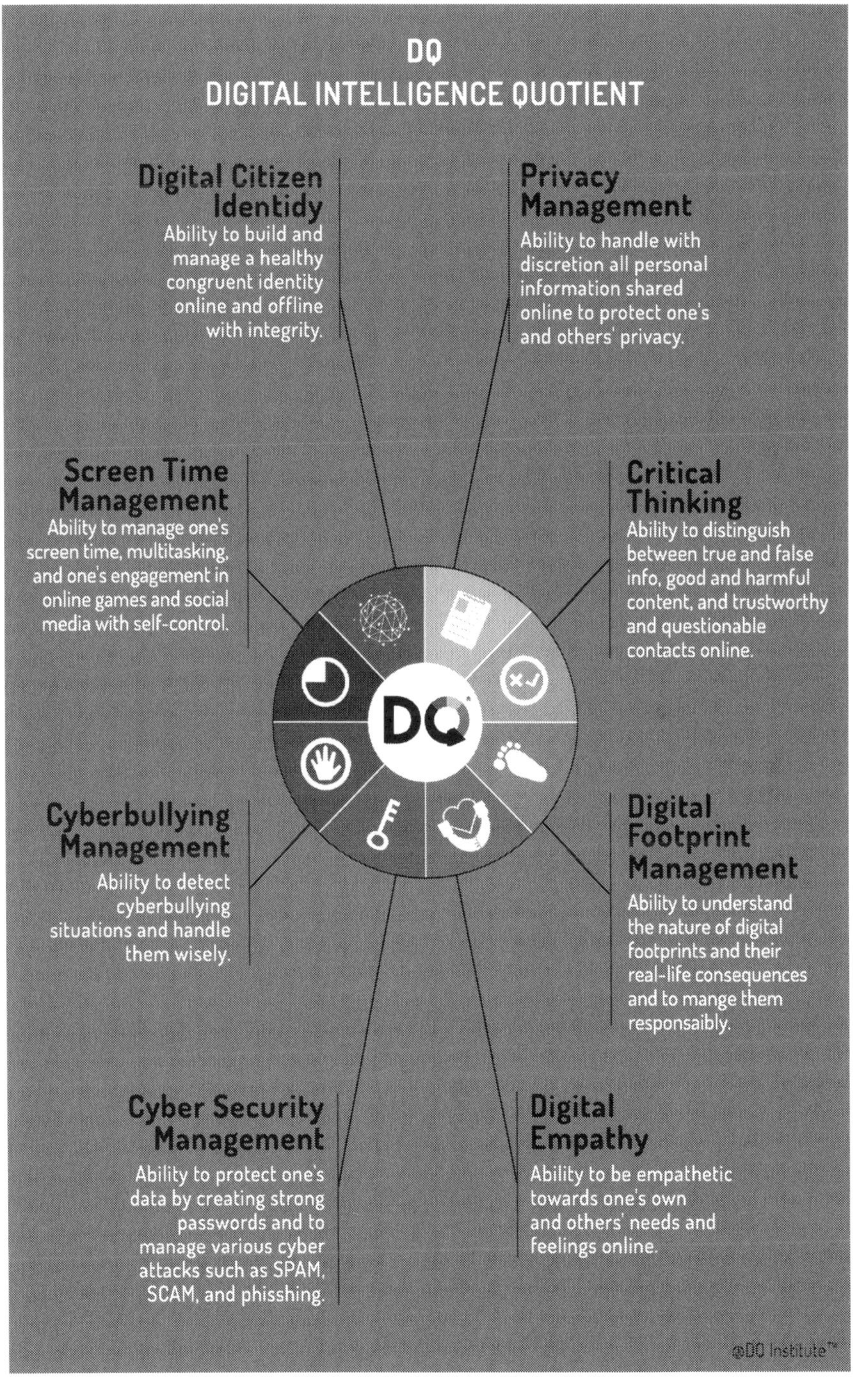
DQ
DIGITAL INTELLIGENCE QUOTIENT
Digital Citizen Identidy
Ability to build and manage a healthy congruent identity online and offline with integrity.
Privacy Management
Ability to handle with discretion all personal information shared online to protect one's and others' privacy.
Screen Time Management
Ability to manage one's screen time, multitasking, and one's engagement in online games and social media with self-control.
Critical Thinking
Ability to distinguish between true and false info, good and harmful content, and trustworthy and questionable contacts online.
DQ
Cyberbullying Management
Ability to detect cyberbullying situations and handle them wisely.
Digital Footprint Management
Ability to understand the nature of digital footprints and their real-life consequences and to mange them responsaibly.
Cyber Security Management
Ability to protect one's data by creating strong passwords and to manage various cyber attacks such as SPAM, SCAM, and phisshing.
Digital Empathy
Ability to be empathetic towards one's own and others' needs and feelings online.
@DQ Institute™

1. DIGITAL CITIZEN IDENTIDY

Ability to build and manage a healthy, congruent identity online and offline with integrity.

> How does the internet work?
> Digital leader creed
> Being a global citizen
> What's my dream?
> Congruent online and offline identities
> Integrity of online persona

2. SCREEN TIME MANAGEMENT

Ability to manage one's screen time, multitasking, and one's engagement in online games and social media with self-control.

> Controlling multi-tasking
> Preventing game addiction
> Harmful effects of excessive screen time
> Self-control in digital use
> Balancing screen time
> Family media rule
> Managing time and priorities

3. CYBERBULLYING MANAGEMENT

Ability to detect cyberbullying situations and handle them wisely.

> Detecting cyber bullying
> What is cyber bullying?

- Identifying types of cyber bullying
- Involvement in cyber bullying unknowingly
- Diffusing a cyber bullying situation
- Who my trusted adults are
- When to seek help

4. CYBER SECURITY MANAGEMENT

Ability to protect one's data by creating strong passwords and to manage various cyber attacks such as SPAM, SCAM, and phisshing.

- Creating strong passwords
- Keeping passwords safe
- Managing SPAM and SCAM
- Manging phising
- Observing mobile security

5. PRIVACY MANAGEMENT

Ability to handle with discretion all personal information shared online to protect one's and others' privacy.

- Personal information
- Keeping privacy on social media
- Protecting others' privacy
- Internet privacy rights
- Balancing screen time

6. CRITICAL THINKING

Ability to distinguish between true and false info, good and harmful content, and trustworthy and questionable contacts online.

> Who do you meet online?
> Who are your online friends?
> The 12 stranger alerts
> How to avoid violent content
> What is inappropriate content?
> How to critique content
> True vs. false info

7. DIGITAL FOOTPRINT MANAGEMENT

Ability to understand the nature of digital footprints and their real-life consequences, and to mange them responsaibly.

> What is digital footprint?
> Digital footprints reveal personal info
> Persistent digital footprints
> Digital footprint impacts digital reputation
> Real life consequences of digital footprints
> Stop. Think. Connect.

5. DIGITAL EMPATHY

Ability to be empathetic towards one's own and others' needs and feelings online.

> Courage to speak up
> By-strangers vs. upstanders

> Listening with empathy online
> Speaking up with empathy
> Empathy for cyber victims
> Not being judgemental online

There is even a test that measures your DQ and compares it with other people's DQ. It has been proven that people with higher DQ are safer on the Internet. If you take a DQ test before and after reading this book, it is very likely that your Digital Intelligence will be higher after the book. One of the goals of this book is to increase your DQ so you can be more successful, happier, and safer in the digital age.

DEFAULT DECISIONS: THE "DO NOTHING" DECISIONS

There is one research in which the difference between the results from Austria and Denmark is huge. Austria gets 99% and Denmark only 4%. Can you imagine what it is?

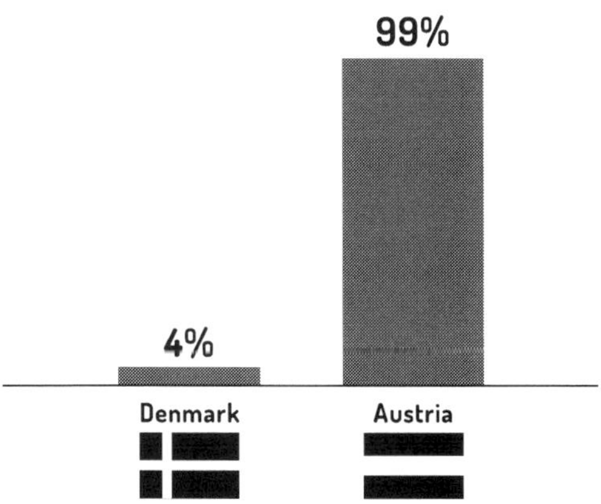

I once asked a group of people in one of my talks what they thought that number represented. Someone shouted: "It's the number of Austrians!" After laughing, even thought that was an interesting answer, I explained it is the percentage of people who are organ donors. And why is that? In Austria, people are automatically organ donors and have to *opt-out* if they don't want to be anymore. In Denmark, they have to *opt-in*.

There is a magic word that influences behaviors: ***default***. Default decisions are the ones made for you when you do nothing. Basically, if you just sit and do nothing, a lot of decisions are made on your behalf.

The default is one of more than 150 known unconscious biases cataloged by Behavioral Economics, a field that has been transforming our view on the way humans make decisions. Behavioraleconomics.com, one of the best online references in the field, explains it as the status quo bias:

> *Status quo bias is evident when people prefer things to stay the same by doing nothing or by sticking with a decision made previously (Samuelson, & Zeckhauser, 1988). This may happen even when only small transition costs are involved and the importance of the decision is great.*[4]

I also find the relationship between the status quo and the concept of inertia fascinating:

> *In behavioral economics, inertia is the endurance of a stable state associated with inaction and the concept of status quo bias. Behavioral nudges*

[4] Status Quo Bias. Behavioral Economics. Available at: <https://www.behavioraleconomics.com/resources/mini-encyclopedia-of-be/status-quo-bias/>. Accessed on: October 10, 2019.

can either work with people's decision inertia (e.g. by setting defaults) or against it (e.g. by giving warnings) (Jung, 2019).

In physics, inertia is the tendency of objects to keep moving at constant speed if no other forces act upon them. For example, if a plane is flying at 500 miles per hour, it tends to keep flying at that very same speed unless something tries to accelerate it or stop it. So, we tend to keep our decisions and not change them unless some force acts upon us.

You should be aware of the decisions that have already been made for you as well as the decisions that you have made previously and not only accept them, but revisit them frequently.

WHAT ARE BIASES?

Unconscious or cognitive biases are systematic errors in the way we think and make decisions. Optical illusions helped me understand biases.

The famous well-known optical illusions are tangible proof that our brain and senses are not perfect. Observe the following image:

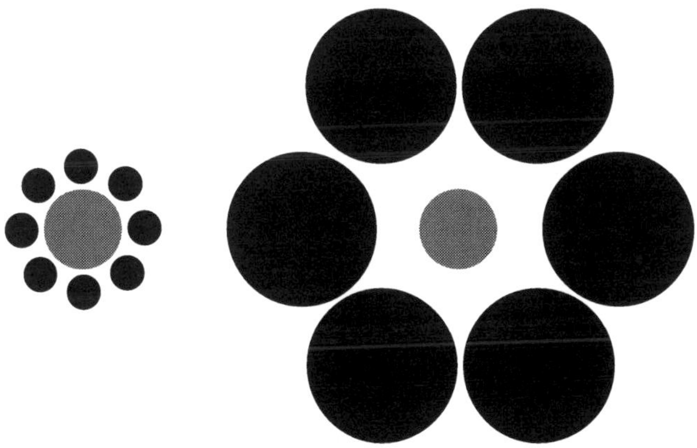

#DigitalNudge

WHAT IS AROUND **INFLUENCES** THE WAY WE SEE THE WORLD AND THE WAY WE MAKE DECISIONS.

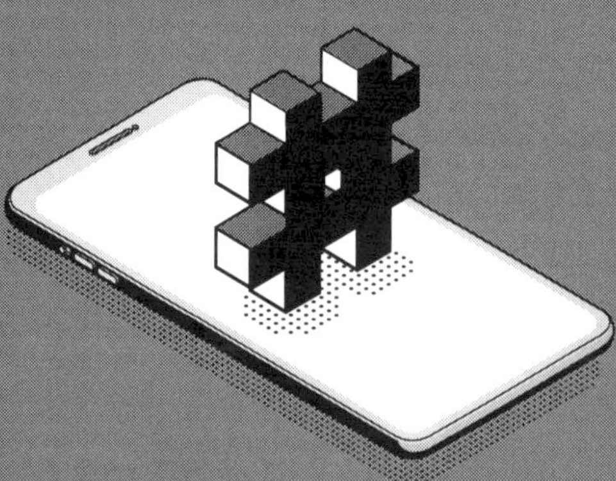

Most people looking at this picture will have the impression that the inner circle on the left is slightly bigger than the one on the right. In fact, though, both are the same size. The "illusion" is caused by the outer circles. On the left, the smaller outer circles make us think the inner one is bigger. Similarly, the bigger outer circles on the right make us think the inner one is smaller. This is a great example that shows that the brain works relatively, not absolutely. Even if we try, we cannot isolate them and look only at the inner circles, ignoring the outer ones. We can only see that the inner circles are the same size when we remove the outer circles. See below:

What is around influences the way we see the world and the way we make decisions.

In optical illusions, we see something different from reality. When we make decisions, biases influence us to consider a limited reality. For decades, scientists, such as Nobel laureate Daniel Kahneman, have been studying and cataloging these biases so we can better understand what they call "human irrationality." Dan Ariely explains in his bestselling book *Predictably Irrational*, through many of his scientific experiments, how the majority of people behave irrationally in a predictable way, how they make the same mistakes, and how it is possible not only to predict but also influence them to act one way or another.

Simple, right? Do you know that online form that says: "Check this box if you don't want to receive our offers by email"? This means that someone has already made the decision for you to receive offers, and if you do not want that, you have to ask to opt-out.

WHAT ARE NUDGES?

The vast majority of our decisions are influenced by irrational factors: lack of attention, lack of full context with all necessary information, emotional factors, etc. There are dozens of unconscious biases that help us understand which factors influence decision-making. In-depth knowledge of these biases makes it possible to create small interventions in the environments in which we make decisions in order to influence people to choose one thing or another. Each one of these interventions is called a *nudge*. The term was coined by Richard Thaler and Cass Sunstein in the book they wrote together, also called *Nudge*. The contributions from behavioral economists are so significant that Thaler won the 2017 Nobel Prize for uniting economics and psychology.

According to Thaler and Sunstein, a nudge is any aspect of the choice architecture that alters people's behavior in a predictable way without forbidding any options or significantly changing their economic incentives. To count as a mere nudge, the intervention must be easy and cheap to avoid. Nudges are not mandates.

These nudges have to be gentle and there must be a clear way to walk away from the decision that the nudge influences a person to make. For example, imagine a parent wants to influence fruit consumption and decrease their children's junk food eating habits:

> It's a *nudge*: if they place the fruit closer to where children play and leave junk food in a cupboard.

NUDGES ARE SMALL AND POWERFUL INTERVENTIONS IN THE ENVIRONMENTS WHERE WE MAKE DECISIONS.

#DigitalNudge

> It is not a *nudge*: if they ban junk food altogether and force children to always eat fruit.

Of course, for other behaviors, the creation of prohibition policies is more effective, such as banning cigarettes in restaurants—which, let's face it, was one of the best decisions humanity has ever made, right?

If you smoke and have a slight feeling of discomfort reading this, I want you to know that this was exactly my intention: this is my nudge for you to stop smoking.

TO COUNT AS
A MERE NUDGE,
THE INTERVENTION
MUST BE EASY
AND CHEAP
TO AVOID.
NUDGES ARE
NOT MANDATES.

#DigitalNudge

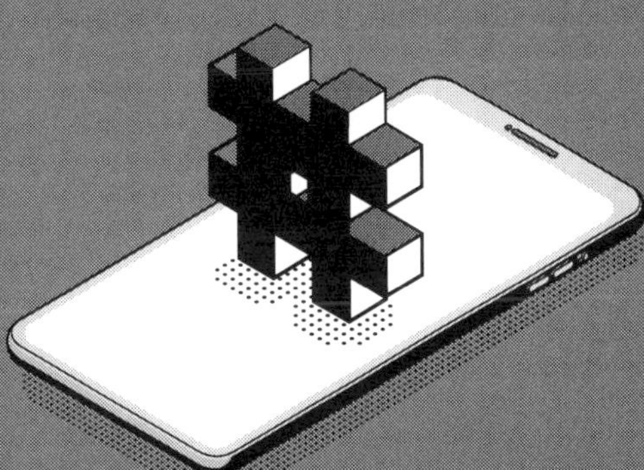

DIGITAL BEHAVIORAL SCIENCE

We spoke of Behavioral Economics, also known as Behavioral Science. From now on, I will use these two terms (Economics and Science) as synonyms. My biggest questions when I started studying Behavioral Science, in 2010 approximately, were:

1. Do the principles of the physical world related to behavioral science also apply to the digital world?
2. If so, how can we correlate and map the forms of physical and digital influence?

The search for answers to these questions using science is what I call Digital Behavioral Science.

DIGITAL DECISION ARCHITECTURE

WHO MAKES THE ARCHITECTURE OF DIGITAL DECISIONS?

In the world of product design and digital interfaces, there is a tremendous power in the hands of UX (User Experience) and XD (Experience Design) people. They have the power to build the digital decision-making environments. And when it's time to decide how to present options to users, their understanding of the way humans make decisions is essential.

A PRACTICAL EXAMPLE

In one of the digital product design teams I worked with, we needed to choose how to introduce options to insurance buyers. Buying insurance is complicated, isn't it? There are many options, coverage for this and that. On our team, for a given product, the buyer could choose 511 different options. To simplify insurance-buying for customers, the team decided to personalize the options. The product would choose the three best buyer package options based on, among other things, a person's job. If they were a photographer, they would see three options; if thet were a businessperson, there would be three other options, something like this:

DIGITAL PERSONALIZATION

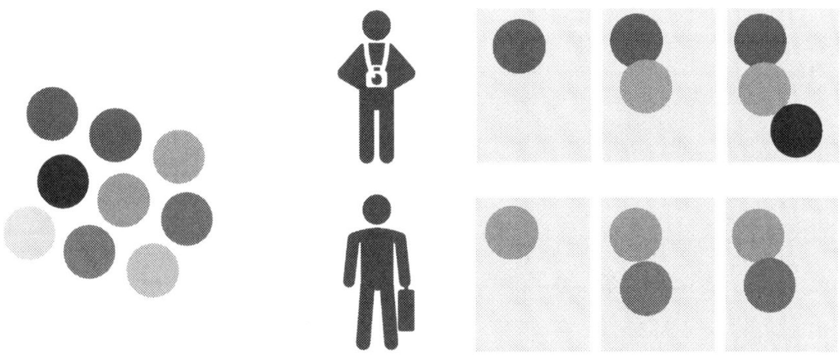

Thus, out of the 511 combo possibilities, buyers could choose three. Of course, after choosing one of these three, other options could be added or removed from the selected "default option." It was almost like going to McDonald's and ordering a Big Mac with no onion: much easier than assembling a whole new burger from scratch.

Speaking of McDonald's, limiting the number of product options was exactly one of the strategies that enabled the chain to scale up, as explained in the movie *The Founder*.[5] But unlike sandwiches, digital products have much greater flexibility. We use a very powerful technique: personalization, which is one of the foundations of smarter digital applications—as Shlomo Benartzi explains in his book *The Smarter Screen*.

Dosage
I (personalization)
Good
Intuitive
Timing
Actionable
Learn

5 *The Founder*, directed by John Lee Hancock. Produced by Jeremy Renner. Weinstein Company, 2016.

POWER AND RESPONSIBILITY

At that moment, on our team, when they personalized three options and the users started choosing them, it became clear to me the immense power people from UX and XD have in their hands. They design where the check-box should be, what will be written next to it, what options should be shown first, and so on. There is great power in deciding the name of the options:

☐ I don't want to receive offers: opt out

☐ I want to receive offers: opt in

And if the options are already checked, everything is reversed:

☑ I don't want to receive offers: opt in

☑ I want to receive offers: opt out

We intuitively think that we only need to "opt out" if something is already selected for us, but design can play with these options in several ways. Got it?

"With great power comes great responsability!" Also known as the Peter Parker principle, this is a popular quote from the *Spider-Man* comic books. For digital product designers, there is a huge responsibility in designing what 4.3 billion internet users,[6] who I call digital citizens, are going to use, so that it addresses a real need rather than simply trying to sell something users don't need or want.

It might be time to start thinking: Do you control your smartphone or does it control you?

[6] KEMP, Simon. Digital 2019: Global Internet Use Accelerates. *We Are Social*, January 30, 2019. Available at: <https://wearesocial.com/blog/2019/01/digital-2019-global-internet-use-accelerates>. Accessed on: October 10, 2019.

DO YOU CONTROL YOUR SMARTPHONE OR DOES IT CONTROL YOU?

#DigitalNudge

THE DIGITAL CONSCIOUSNESS PYRAMID

One of the goals of this book is to raise your digital consciousness. How can you know at what level you are? The pyramid below has four levels.

DIGITAL CONSCIOUSNESS PYRAMID

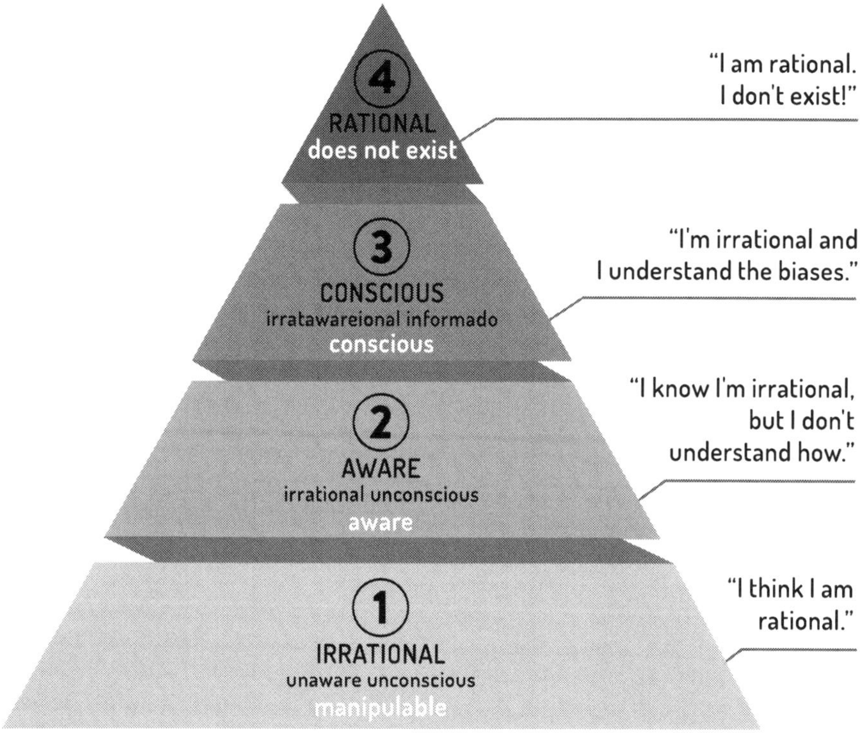

LEVEL 1 "I THINK I AM RATIONAL"

At level 1 you are irrational, unaware, and unconscious. But because you are unaware, you believe many things that are actually not true. You believe you are completely rational, you believe you are not influenced, and you believe you make your own decisions. It turns out that when you move to level 2, you will review most of these beliefs.

LEVEL 2 "I KNOW I'M IRRATIONAL, BUT I DON'T UNDERSTAND HOW"

At level 2 you are still irrational, because we all are, but you are already aware of your irrationality. You are still unconscious, so you are irrational, aware, and unconscious. The only thing that changes from Level 1 to Level 2 is your attitude towards knowing and accepting your irrationality. Therefore, the statement that represents this level is: "I know I'm irrational, but I don't understand how." You still don't understand because you still don't know the cognitive biases, the traps that influence most of your decisions. You know you are irrational, you know you're influenced, but you still don't understand how that happens.

LEVEL 3 "I AM IRRATIONAL AND I UNDERSTAND THE BIASES"

At level 3 you are still irrational, because we all are, but you are already aware and now, most importantly, you are conscious of your irrationality. You know and understand unconscious biases, sometimes identify when you are being influenced, but sometimes you are still influenced, as it is impossible for us to completely overcome the essence of human irrationality and be 100% rational. So, there is Level 4, which is merely representative.

LEVEL 4 "I AM RATIONAL, I DO NOT EXIST!"

At level 4 you are totally rational, have no cognitive bias, have endless attention, and all the information in the world to make the best decisions ever. Which means: you do not exist! You would be what Thaler and Sunstein call *econs* in the book *Nudge*:

> *People who behave exactly as described by economists are also called the* Homo economicus. *They have perfect rationality, in the economic sense that their preferences are consistent and they always take actions that maximize their own satisfaction and interest.*

So, at what level are you? It is very likely that after reading this book, you will be almost at level 3, which is the highest level a human being can reach!

#DigitalNudge

DIGITAL CONSCIOUSNESS IS NOT ABOUT NOT USING YOUR SMARTPHONE, IT IS ABOUT NOT LETTING IT USE YOU.

SOME EXAMPLES OF DIGITAL NUDGES

There are several strategies to influence someone to choose, buy, sign in, subscribe, order, submit, accept, search or click in the digital world. One of the most powerful is the digital default, the decision that technology, or someone behind technology, has already made for you and which, if you do nothing, it will become your decision. Here are some examples of digital defaults and other nudges, as well as how they might appear in your life in the digital world.

BOXES, BULLETS, AND ARROWS

In the tech world, these are also known as checkboxes, radio buttons, and dropdowns. It is always important to understand what happens if you do nothing, neither check nor uncheck. You may have already seen one of them in some form or application you were using:

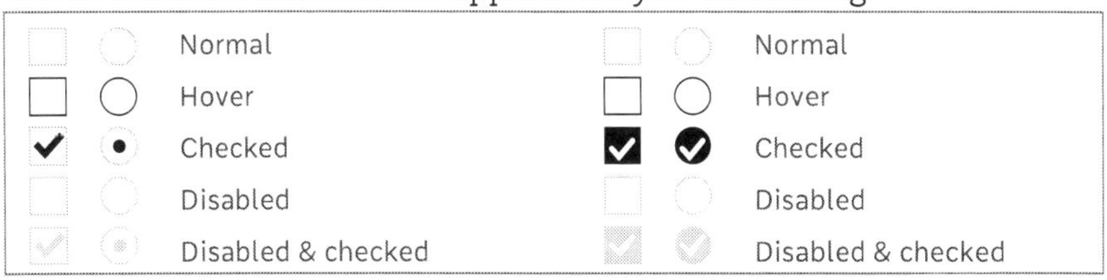

An increasing number of buttons and digital interfaces already populated keep appearing:

Every time you come across one of these, you can be sure that there is a decision already made for you. If already checked, you need to uncheck it if you want to opt out. If it is not checked, you need to decide whether you want to check it and opt in. That is, doing nothing means accepting what has already been decided—the default option or digital default. Decide consciously.

When you come across a checkbox already checked or unchecked, or such a radio button, ask yourself: "What if I do nothing? If I don't check or uncheck and do absolutely nothing, what decision will I be making?"

#DigitalNudge

"WHAT IF I DO NOTHING? IF I DON'T CHECK OR UNCHECK AND DO ABSOLUTELY NOTHING, WHAT DECISION WILL I BE MAKING?"

#DigitalNudge

9 OUT OF 10 PEOPLE CHOOSE A RESULT FROM THE FIRST PAGE.

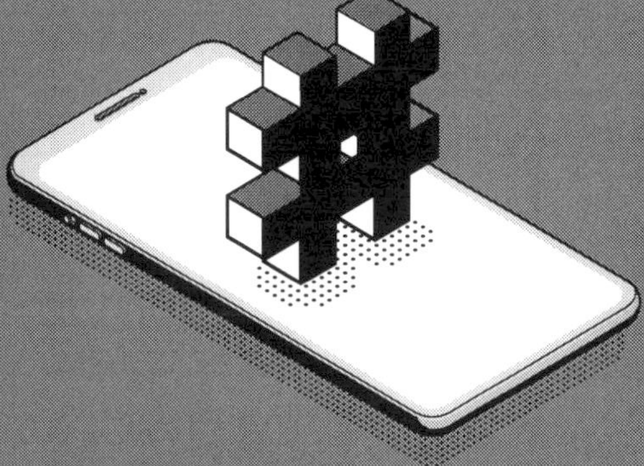

SEARCH RESULTS

If we go to Google now and search for "where to eat in New York", it will show over 300 million results. Which one do you click? It is important to know that 9 out of 10 people choose a result from the first page.

In other words, was it you who chose the place to eat or was it Google? The results from the first page are a nudge to click on one of them. Of course, in an ideal world where the main goal is to help digital citizens who are looking for something, the results would come in order of relevance and those on the first page would be guaranteed to be the most relevant to the person searching.

But is the goal of helping users always a priority in all digital products? Let's start with the fact that the first results that appear are "sponsored links," i.e., people or companies that paid to appear on this list. So, relevance is already based on who paid the most and not on which link is really relevant or will satisfy your needs as a user of that search.

Try going to other result pages other than the first one when searching for something. Check if the results are relevant to you. Don't get stuck just on the first page. Search consciously!

PRESELECTED OPTIONS

When Uber launched the "pool" option, passengers were able to share their trip with others in order to lower the cost. Interestingly, Uber decided to select this option for me automatically. One day, I opened the app and the pool option was already selected. I had never seen this option and there it was, new and already selected.

I love talking to Uber drivers. One of them told me a story of an old lady who ordered an Uber pool and when she got to the car and saw there was another passenger, she wondered for a few seconds and questioned the driver what was happening. The driver looked at her and replied: "You got an Uber pool." And she said: "I ordered what?!"

She decided to use that product feature without even knowing what she was choosing. She did it because it was already checked for her as a default and preselected option on the app. Was it her who made that decision or was it Uber itself that chose the pool option when she got a car, without looking at the previously checked option?

Before clicking on action buttons to proceed, such as the "Confirm" button on Uber, you should pay attention to which options are already selected for you and should decide for yourself if you want these options that way. The decisions have to be yours! Order consciously!

TIMELINES AND FEEDS

If you use Facebook, Instagram, LinkedIn, Twitter or some other social media app where you keep scrolling through infinite posts which seem to never end, then welcome to the world of "timelines," also known as feeds. The list contains various things like posts from people you follow, pages you like, sponsored posts, and more.

Scrolling feels like we're using a slot machine, doesn't it? As Tristan Harris said: "If you're an app, how do you keep people hooked? Turn yourself into a slot machine. The average person checks their phone 150 times a day. Why do we do this? Are we making 150 conscious choices?" Tristan was called the "closest thing Silicon Valley has to

#DigitalNudge

BEFORE CLICKING ON ACTION BUTTONS TO PROCEED, YOU SHOULD PAY ATTENTION TO WHICH OPTIONS ARE ALREADY SELECTED FOR YOU AND SHOULD DECIDE FOR YOURSELF IF YOU WANT THESE OPTIONS THAT WAY. THE DECISION HAS TO BE YOURS!

a conscience."[7] He spent three years as a Google Design Ethicist developing a framework for how technology should "ethically" steer the thoughts and actions of billions of people from screens. He is now co-founder of the Center for Humane Technology, whose mission is to reverse "human downgrading" and re-align technology with humanity.

Have you ever been in a situation where a friend of yours who you follow on one of these apps posted something and it never appeared on your timeline? I just have logged in to Facebook, and the first post was from a friend who had posted two hours ago, while the second was from a friend who had posted nine hours ago. I keep asking myself: "During these seven hours, has no other friend of mine posted anything?" It is very likely that other friends have posted within this seven hours interval, but these posts did not appear on my timeline.

This is due to fact that, as more friends keeping posting, more pages are being followed, and more posts are being sponsored, the timeline has to decide in which order to show what you follow. This decision is not always made based only on time, i.e. showing first the most recent ones. There are several other factors that must be considered for something to appear or not in your feed.

A *TechCrunch* article—"Why Is Facebook Page Reach Decreasing?" —explains that the number of possible posts to be displayed per day for each user varies from 1,500 to 15,000. In other words, there are up to 15,000 options for which posts to display daily on a timeline. The

[7] HARRIS, Tristan. How Technology is Hijacking Your Mind – from a Magician and Google Design Ethicist. Medium, May 18, 2016. Available at: <https://medium.com/thrive-global/how-technology-hijacks-peoples-minds-from-a-magician-and-google-s-design-ethicist-56d62ef5edf3>. Accessed on: October 10, 2019.

image below explains a bit of the factors Facebook takes into account when deciding whether a post will appear on your timeline.

NEWS FEED VISIBILITY = I (interest) × P (post) × C (creator) × T (typo) × R (recency)

Source: TechCrunch. *Available at:* <*https://techcrunch.com/2014/04/03/the-filtered-feed-problem/*>. *Accessed on* October 10, 2019.

The formula includes:

- Interest of the user in the creator;
- This post's performance amongst other users;
- Performance of past post by the content creator amongst other user;
- Type of post (status, photo, link) user prefer;
- How recent the post is;

It is important to remember that, as the image also states, "this is a simplified equation. Facebook also looks at about 100,000 other high-personalized factors when determining what's shown."

Do you decide what to see on your timelines or do Facebook, Instagram, LinkedIn and all the other digital timeline environments nudge you to consume the content they find most relevant to you?

We have already seen that Facebook has a formula that defines what you will see on your timeline, but according to Behavioral Economics and the nudge theory, it should be easy to "opt out" and choose our own filters. Once you made a decision and there is no option to "opt out," it stops being a nudge and becomes an obligation. It should be possible to say: "I want to sort my timeline by time, close friends, subject, just photos or videos." Unfortunately, we don't have all this control over social media filters. It's like going to an all-you-can-eat restaurant thinking you're going to have the right to choose what to eat, in what order you want food to be served, but having to accept the dishes that are brought in the sequence the restaurant decides, and moreover, not being able to say you don't want something that has already been served. Can you imagine this situation? Would you go to a restaurant like this?

In the case of timelines, some social media give us the option to configure and "prioritize" what we want to see. Facebook, for example, lets us select friends and pages we want to prioritize; it's the option "See First."

So, take control of your timelines! Go to Facebook and other social media preferences to prioritize who and what you think is important. Choose a dozen people and pages you want to pay more attention to and see what you want, not just what a magic formula that someone else decided would be best for you! Scroll consciously!

STREAKS: EVERY SINGLE DAY

"I've been doing this for thirty years every single day, and I'm not addicted." This quote became famous in the video *Tapa na Pantera*,[8] a fictional performance in which an actress says she has been smoking weed for thirty years, "every single day" and is not addicted. Do you think someone who has been doing something for thirty years

[8] Video *Tapa na Pantera* (2006). Available at: <https://www.youtube.com/watch?v=6rMloi>. Accessed on: May 5, 2019.

#DigitalNudge

SO, TAKE CONTROL OF YOUR **TIMELINES!** GO TO FACEBOOK AND OTHER SOCIAL MEDIA PREFERENCES TO **PRIORITIZE** WHO AND WHAT YOU THINK IS **IMPORTANT**.

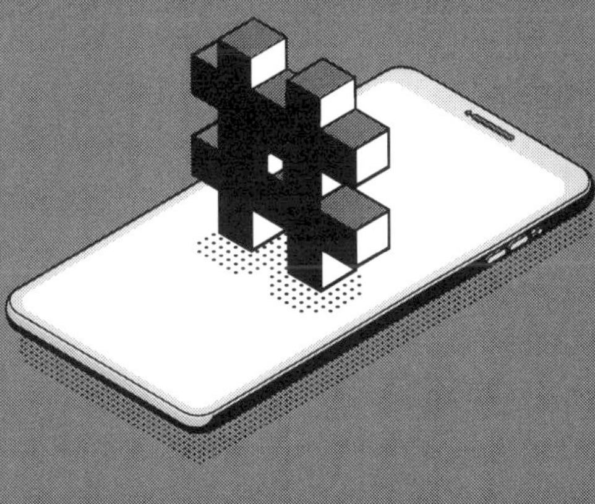

every single day is addicted? I imagine your answer might be along the lines of: "It depends what it is that they have been doing".

How do we form a habit of doing something every single day? Like brushing our teeth, bathing or meditating every single day. One very clever solution created by the powerful digital product designers are the streaks. What is a streak? To explain it, let's take Snapchat as an example. If you thought "Snap what?," it might be useful to start with an explanation of what Snapchat is—and I want to thank the portal *Make Use Of* for writing such an amazing and simple "What is Snapchat" article:

> *Snapchat is a multimedia app that can be used on smartphones running Android or iOS. It allows you to send pictures or videos, named "Snaps," to friends. These Snaps vanish after they've been viewed. The platform also offers a Chat function, similar to instant messaging services like WhatsApp. The main difference, however, is that, as with Snaps, Chats disappear once they've been viewed. You can change your settings so Chats vanish 24 hours after opening instead. They can also be saved by tapping once on the message; either user in the conversation can delete Chats by tapping again. Nonetheless, the whole point of Snapchat is that anything sent, soon disappears.*[9]

Another interesting piece of information about Snapchat is that Facebook tried to buy it in 2013 for 3 billion dollars, and Google has also tried to acquire it in 2016 for 30 billion dollars, but none of them

---

[9] BATES, Philip. What Is Snapchat. Make Use Of, March 27, 2019. Available at: <https://www.makeuseof.com/tag/what-is-snapchat/>, Accessed on: October 10, 2019.

were able to close the deal during those attempts. Facebook has adapted some of Snapchat's features to their social networks, including the famous "stories," which is one of the most commonly used features on Instagram.

Going back to streaks, one of Snapchat's features is called snapstreaks. They are represented by a fire icon and a number next to it, as the image below shows:

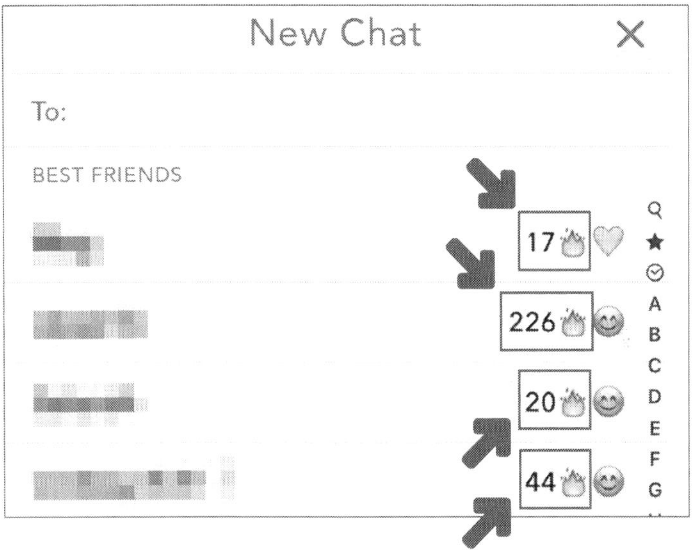

The Snapchat support site explains what this means: "You are on a Snapstreak if you and your friend have Snapped (not chatted) each other within 24 hours for more than three consecutive days. The number next to the fire icon tells you how many days you've been on a Snapstreak. For example, if you have an 8 next to the fire icon it means you both have Snapped back and forth with this friend for 8 days."[10]

[10] Available at: <https://support.snapchat.com/en-GB/a/snapstreaks>. Accessed on: October 10, 2019.

In the image above, one of the streaks has the number 226. It means that these two people are sending snaps to each other every single day for 226 days. If one of the two does not send a snap, the streak resets! That's right: It goes back to zero and you have to start all over again.

The shocking *Business Insider* article "Teens Are Obsessed with this One Snapchat Score that Can Make or Break Friendships" shows how streaks influence young people: "'I've definitely heard people use Snapchat streaks as a kind of measurement for how close they are with someone,' said Eve, student. 'For example: if someone's name comes up in a conversation, I've heard people say things like "oh yeah, I love her, we have a 200 day Snapchat streak."'" Testimonies from teenagers and from several other online sources show how Snapchat streaks influence the application use and engagement.

Another app that also uses streaks to encourage and influence people to use it "every single day" is Duolingo. It is the world's largest free language learning site and it also uses streaks to engage people who are studying through the platform. Much like Snapchat streaks, Duolingo streaks are also represented by a "fire icon" and a number. The number represents how many days the user has reached their daily goal, called XP Goal. This mechanism is explained in more detail in the Duolingo support article "What Is a Streak?"[11]

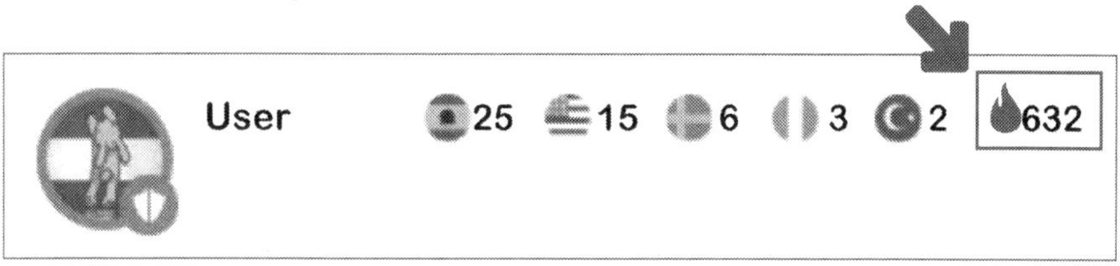

[11] Available at: <https://support.duolingo.com/hc/en-us/articles/204980880-What-is-a-streak->. Accessed on: May 5, 2019.

Snapchat and Duolingo are two examples of how streaks can influence behavior to increase the frequency of digital application usage, in the "every single day" routine. The streaks are a great example of a digital nudge that influences our decisions and daily behaviors, helping to create and keep daily habits.

DOPAMINE AND LOSS AVERSION EXPLAIN THE POWER OF STREAKS

The reasons behind this secret streak influencing force can be explained in two ways: gain and loss. Pleasure of gaining and fear of losing. Increasing and maintaining streaks is like a game to our brain. With each passing day, we advance a phase and earn a number. Pete Brown says in his article "The Power of the Streaks" that his daughter has been talking to him less because she uses the time they spend going to school together to "keep her streaks." Pete suggests that each time a person replies to her daughter's message and she "keeps the streak" for another day, her brain releases dopamine. Simon Sinek also explains this in an interview that went viral:

"WE KNOW WHEN YOU GET THE ATTENTION IT FEELS GOOD, YOU GET A HIT OF DOPAMINE WHICH FEELS GOOD, WHICH IS WHY WE KEEP GOING BACK TO IT. DOPAMINE IS THE EXACT

SAME CHEMICAL THAT MAKES US FEEL GOOD WHEN WE SMOKE, WHEN WE DRINK, AND WHEN WE GAMBLE. IN OTHER WORDS, IT'S HIGHLY, HIGHLY ADDICTIVE."[12]

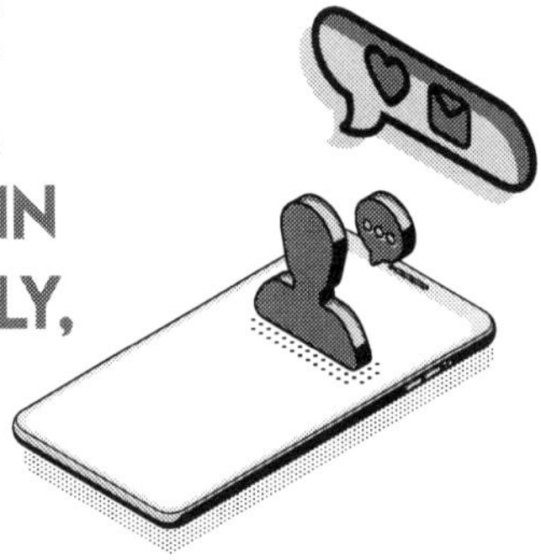

Looking at the situation from the eyes of Behavioral Economics and of human irrationality, it suggests that the fear of losing a streak is greater than the pleasure of dopamine released when we keep a streak. Remember the cognitive biases? The mistakes that make us think and make irrational decisions I explained earlier? Loss aversion is one of the overpowering cognitive biases that influence our behavior.

What is loss aversion? One of our main sources on this sort of knowledge, the website behavioraleconomics.com, explains the scientific work of Amos Tversky and Kahneman: "It is thought that the pain of losing is psychologically about twice as powerful as the pleasure of gaining. People are more willing to take risks to avoid a loss than to make a gain."[13] We are very afraid of losing anything that seems to belong to us, and this fear makes us act irrationally.

Sam, a student interviewed by *Business Insider*, endorses once again that the science of irrational human behavior is right. Sam stated:

---

12 YOUTUBE. Simon Sinek on Millennials in The Workplace. Available at: <www.youtube.com/watch?v=hER0Qp6QJNU>. Accessed on: May 9,2019.

13 Loss aversion. Behavioral Economics. Available at: <https://www.behavioraleconomics.com/resources/mini-encyclopedia-of-be/loss-aversion/>. Accessed on: October 10, 2019.

"I hate streaks because it forces you to be on your phone every day. Say you have a 100-day streak. There's a lot of obligation to continue. So if you lose your streak, it's like the world's over." Pay attention to the words used by Sam: hate, obligation, lose. All these words lead us to the loss aversion bias. To say that "it's like the world's over" because a simple number has been reset to zero on your phone is amazing, isn't it? This is the power of the loss aversion bias leveraged by the digital world through a tool called streaks, a powerful digital nudge.

Of course, we know that the video *Tapa na Pantera* is a fictional work only used here at the beginning of this section to make things a bit funnier. However, if the video with the actress smoking weed had a streak, it would have a fire icon with the number 10,950 next to it, representing her over thirty years of use "every single day." A streak of over 10,000, and she still says she's "not addicted", what do you think about that?

VIRTUAL REALITY (VR) AND AUGMENTED REALITY (AR)

Virtual Reality (VR) and Augmented Reality (AR) are two of the most powerful emerging technologies to influence people. Imagine you are immersed in a completely different environment than you are now. The power of the people who create this environment is even greater than a simple button or checkbox.

Research conducted at the Stanford Virtual Human Interaction Lab (VHIL), in Stanford, is experimenting on how VR and AR can be used to deconstruct stereotypes, reduce racism, and increase empathy among people. One of the experiments is called Minorities Mirror, where people can "put themselves in someone else's shoes" and see themselves in a mirror within a virtual environment. The experiments are done with different groups of people and genders. Imagine a white woman who suddenly finds herself in the body of a black man in a virtual environment. Then another person arrives and begins to say offensive things about the traits they see in the mirror. Years of research have shown that situations like this increase the level of empathy related to certain groups of people. Kenneth Seward Jr. talked about this in his article "How Virtual Reality Can Be Used to Fight Racism and Prejudice in Society": "As the virtual reality industry continues to evolve though, it can be used to help people see things from the perspective of a minority in America. You know, wear someone else's shoes and all that. This sort of thing has helped people see past their own experiences".[14]

PERSUASION AND COERCION: THE TWO TYPES OF INFLUENCE

You have been introduced to some digital nudges. But consider saying this to yourself: *I am making a digital decision now. Has anyone already decided for me while designing this app? Do I need to ask to opt out?*

Understanding human behavior has led many digital products to create mechanisms of dependency on their users. But is this dependency good? Nir Eyal, author of *Hooked*, speaks of two types of influence: persuasion and coercion.

[14] Available at: <https://uploadvr.com/vr-fight-racism-prejudice/>. Accessed on: October 10, 2019.

#DigitalNudge

2 TYPES OF INFLUENCE

PERSUASION

Influencing people to do what they **want and need**.

COERSION

Influencing people to do what they **don't want and don't need**

- **Persuasion:** influencing people to do what they want and need.
- **Coercion:** influencing people to do what they don't want and don't need.

In early 2018, Facebook creator and CEO Mark Zuckerberg testified in front of the US Congress with special regard to data usage and respect for user privacy amid the Cambridge Analytica scandal, which has affected millions of people worldwide.

Zuckerberg owned up to the mistakes before the US Congress, and two of his statements were relevant to understanding how the digital world can influence people: "We didn't take a broad enough view of our responsibility, and that was a big mistake. And it was my mistake. And I'm sorry. I started Facebook, I run it, and I'm responsible for what happens here."[15]

Of course, the mistake is never solely of one person, but Zuckerberg took responsibility for his company. It's important that all digital world designers keep this in mind! Mark also stated: "Across the board, we have a responsibility to not just build tools, but to make sure that they're used for good."

DARK PATTERNS: WHEN THE INTERNET MANIPULATES US

The Internet manipulates you when it uses coercion techniques to influence you to do things you don't want and don't need. Harry Brignull

[15] Available at: <https://www.youtube.com/watch?v=IOg7QEE1uEQ>. Accessed on: October 10, 2019.

defines coercion patterns as "dark patterns." On his website,[16] there are lists of strategies that web pages and other digital products use to deceive users. Here are some examples to watch out for and not fall into the pitfalls of digital manipulation:

> **Forced Continuity:** When your free trial with a service comes to an end and your credit card silently starts getting charged without any warning. In some cases, this is made even worse by making it difficult to cancel the membership.

> **Sneak into Basket:** You attempt to purchase something, but somewhere in the purchasing journey the site sneaks an additional item into your basket, often through the use of an opt-out radio button or checkbox on a prior page.

> **Friend Spam:** The product asks for your email or social media permissions under the pretense that it will be used for a desirable outcome (e.g. finding friends), but then spams all your contacts in a message that claims to be from you.

These are just a few of my favorite examples, all of which are explained on www.darkpatterns.org. In order to raise your digital consciousness, you should make yourself aware of these dark patterns and try to identify them when you are navigating digitally. It is very likely you'll find some of them.

---

16 DARK PARTTERNS. What are dark patterns? Available at: <https://www.darkpatterns.org/>. Accessed on: May 5, 2019.

#DIGITALNUDGES4GOOD

But there is light at the end of the tunnel! Part of the #DigitalNudge movement is about understanding that the best nudge is the one that helps a person do what already needs to be done. This is what we call understanding and addressing a user need.

When I worked as a Digital Transformation Adviser for the Digital Transformation Agency at the Australian Government, we all collaboratively helped develop what was called the Digital Service Standard. The Digital Service Standard is made up of thirteen criteria to help government agencies design and deliver services that are simple, clear and fast. It was quite important for us that the first of the thirteen criteria was "Understand user needs; research to develop a deep knowledge of the users and their context for using the service."

Here I want to highlight a few digital nudge strategies that really looked at addressing user needs.

DIGITAL NUDGES THAT HELP PEOPLE WITH DIABETES

According to the website *Quin Tech*, one in every twelve people in the world has diabetes, which amounts to 415 million people. It is estimated that around 1.3 trillion dollars are spent each year on treatment.

My friend Greg has diabetes—I learned from him that I should not say that he is "diabetic" but that he "has diabetes" because the condition does not define him. A few years ago, he told me that when he attended important meetings, he could rarely focus because he was always "paying attention" to what he was feeling, for example, if he was dizzy or tired. These were signs that he needed to be monitoring

THERE IS AN APP THAT MAKES DECISIONS FOR PEOPLE WITH DIABETES AND THE MORE THE APP DECIDES, THE BETTER IT GETS.

#DigitalNudge

to know the right time to take insulin. By paying attention to these signals, Greg focused less on the meeting; since our attention is limited, we cannot pay attention to many things at once—this is one of the limitations that Behavioral Economics teaches us.

I was in a meeting with Greg and he told me that he no longer needs to "waste his attention" watching the signals. Now, he uses a device called Continuous Glucose Monitoring (CGM) and, when his glucose level is low or high, he gets a notification on his smartphone. Hence, he no longer needs to waste his attention on the signals and make for himself the decision to take insulin. He has delegated this decision to a digital device that makes the decision for him. Now, Greg uses his focus on more creative things.

Another example came from Isabella Degen, a robotic engineer specializing in Machine Learning (ML) and Artificial Intelligence (AI). Isabella was diagnosed with diabetes as a child and said: "Like many of you, I spend my days calculating, monitoring, analyzing, recalling, waiting, and worrying about the impact that every meal, activity and emotion will have on my body. For many years, I've dreamed of offloading all this to a machine."[17] Isabella founded, along with Cyndi Williams, Quin Tech,[18] formerly known as Ayuda Heuristics, a company that aims to challenge fundamental beliefs about the definition, diagnosis, and management of diabetes and to bring new solutions. Quin Tech is a #DigitalNudge4Good.

17 Available at: <https://medium.com/quintechdotio/from-us-7247c4d5ca38>. Accessed on: October 10, 2019.

18 Learn more at: <https://quintech.io/>. Accessed on: May 15, 2019.

It all starts when you download the app, Quin, and then it tries to help you with your treatment by suggesting, trying, making mistakes, getting it right, and learning from mistakes and successes. Yes, that's right, the app learns over time. This is exactly what we call "machine learning," when computers, applications, and smartphones are able to improve themselves. And they learn fast.

You're making hundreds of self-care decisions a day. Quin aims to make that quicker and easier. Here's how:

> You log your decisions by taking pictures of what you eat and drink, and logging your insulin doses.
> Quin makes sure other data is logged for you, using your smartphone and your CGM.
> Quin calculates what may be affecting your blood glucose in the moment you need to make a decision, and recalls what's worked for you in the past.

Quin believes the most reliable way to decide how much insulin to take is to recall a decision you've made in the past and reiterate it. The app helps you do that, making quicker decisions by automatically calculating your best past decision, considering everything it knows about your current situation.

Quin's founders say the goal of the app is to make as many decisions as possible so you don't have to worry or think about when and how to act, no matter where you are or what you're doing. In other words, an application that acts for you. Sounds like a science fiction movie, doesn't it? But it is reality, and it exists today!

DIGITAL NUDGES THAT HELP PREVENT CAR CRASHES

In 2006, I was driving back home and was very sleepy. The ride took almost an hour, and all the way I tried really hard not to fall asleep. I turned up the music, danced, slapped my own cheek and said to myself: "You can't sleep, Fabio!" When I was about five minutes from my destination, bang! I fell asleep and woke up after the crash. The front car driver came to me shouting, very angry. I explained that I had fallen asleep, that I was very tired, that I was working hard, and I apologized. No one got hurt, I contacted my insurance company, and everything was all right. Unfortunately, however, not everyone who undergoes a situation like this has the same ending. Car accident statistics in the US show that 40% of road accidents are caused by tired drivers. In the United States alone, there are about 6 million accidents a year, with more than 90 deaths every day.[19]

Smart Cap is a technology that eliminates these so-called "microsleeps." What they call LifeBand uses state of the art brainwave technology to determine a driver's alertness and eliminate microsleeps with accurate fatigue measurements. It is one of the so-called wearables, or wearable technology. Through brainwave reading, this technology identifies when the driver is about to have a microsleep, and then comes the digital nudge that helps the driver stay awake, preventing a possible accident. Really smart, don't you think? Smart Cap is a #DigitalNudge4Good.

[19] Available at: <https://www.driverknowledge.com/car-accident-statistics/>. Accessed on: October 10, 2019.

Ford SafeCap is a similar project. The aim of this wearable is to promote safe driving by monitoring head movement and emitting vibrations to prevent truck drivers from falling asleep while behind the wheel. They conducted research to identify which movements are part of the trucker's work routine and which are related to sleep. This study (behavior analysis) was applied to the software installed on the cap, which alerts the driver with sound, light, and vibration when noticing a sleep behavior—the digital nudges. SafeCap is a #DigitalNudge4Good.[20]

From the eyes of Digital Nudge, the most amazing thing about Smart Cap and SafeCap is that they use different technology to address the same user need—prevent drivers from falling asleep while driving. If you're working with technology, what need does it address?

[20] Available at: <https://bolha.com.br/work/ford-safe-cap/>. Accessed on: October 10, 2019.

CLICKING FAST AND SLOW

A BAT, A BALL, AND OUR TWO BRAINS

Try to solve the following quiz by thinking fast:

> You have a bat and a ball.

> The bat and the ball together cost $1.10.

> The bat costs one dollar more than the ball.

> How much does the ball cost?

If the first answer that came to your mind was: "The ball costs 10 cents," think a little bit longer. If the ball price were 10 cents, the bat, which is one dollar more expensive, would be $1.10. In this case, the sum of the two would be $1.20. It is known, however, that the sum of the two is actually $1.10. That means the right answer to how much does the ball cost is 5 cents, right?

Don't feel bad if you made that mistake, as half the students from some of the best universities in the world (Harvard, Princeton, and MIT) gave the same answer. In fact, this happens when we think fast. In *Thinking Fast and Slow*, Daniel Kahneman explains how our brain has two systems: one that makes quick but not very accurate decisions, and one that is slower but more accurate.

Here's a description of the two systems:

> System 1: Fast, automatic, frequent, emotional, stereotypic, unconscious. Examples (in order of complexity) of things system 1 can do:
  - determine that an object is at a greater distance than another;
  - localize the source of a specific sound;
  - complete the phrase "war and ...";
  - display disgust when seeing a gruesome image;
  - solve 2+2= ?;
  - read text on a billboard;
  - drive a car on an empty road;
  - come up with a good chess move (if you're a chess master);
  - understand simple sentences;
  - connect the description "quiet and structured person with an eye for details" to a specific job.

> System 2: Slow, demanding, infrequent, logical, calculating, conscious. Examples of things system 2 can do:
  - brace yourself before the start of a sprint;
  - direct your attention towards the clowns at the circus;
  - direct your attention towards someone at a loud party;
  - look out for the woman with the grey hair;
  - dig into your memory to recognize a sound;
  - sustain a higher than normal walking rate;

- determine the appropriateness of a particular behavior in a social setting;
- count the number of A's in a certain text;
- give someone your phone number;
- park into a tight parking space;
- determine the price/quality ratio of two washing machines;
- determine the validity of a complex logical reasoning;
- solve 17 × 24.[21]

Both systems are required to make everyday life more efficient. Imagine if you needed to think slowly every time you did something like walking, brushing your teeth or driving. It is important to be aware of which one to use depending on the occasion and type of activity that will be performed. The biggest risk is making decisions using the fast brain when you should be using the slow one.

AN IMPEACHMENT, AN INVASION, A NANNY

Did you know that on December 9, 2016 the President of South Korea, Park Geun-hye, was impeached? Most people I ask say they didn't know or didn't remember. However, when I show them the following image, most of them do remember it.

[21] Available at: <https://en.wikipedia.org/wiki/Thinking,_Fast_and_Slow#Two_systems>. Accessed on October 10, 2019.

Image of Professor Robert Kelly in a BBC interview[22]

The image shows Professor Robert Kelly giving an interview from his home to the *BBC News UK*. It was meant to be just an interview about the impeachment, but Marion, Kelly's daughter, walked into her father's office dancing, unaware of the seriousness of that interview—because, of course, she was only 4. As Marion dances alongside her father, who tries to ignore her presence and continues giving the interview as if nothing was happening, James, his other 8 month-old son, also enters the room on his baby walker. Soon after, a woman quickly goes in to take the children out so the interview would continue.

As the internet never forgives, or rather, people who use the Internet do not miss a chance, after this episode, Twitter was full of messages about the children's entry into the interview. A tweet said: "Immigrant nanny probably got chewed out/fired. He stiff-armed his daughter like nothing so you know he yelled at that woman afterwards."

Followed by: "This nanny is absolutely unemployed."

And: "Ha-ha-ha! The nanny coming in like a ninja and trying to leave unseen is priceless, the best part!!!"

[22] Available at: <https://www.youtube.com/watch?v=0M7679g1BEw>. Accessed on: May 5, 2019.

Then the tweets took another turn after the following response: "You realize the level of stereotype when people automatically say the woman is the nanny because she's Asian."

In fact, the woman who entered the room is Jung-a Kim, former yoga teacher, mother of the children, and professor Kelly's wife. According to the *BBC*, she and Kelly were married shortly after the specialist moved to South Korea.

It was clear that at this point people were tweeting using their troublesome, stereotypical, and fast-paced (system 1) brain that makes many mistakes. Jung-a Kim was wrongly categorized as "the nanny" when, in fact, she is "the mother."

But why did people think she was the nanny and not the children's mother? The *BBC article* "Why Did People Assume an Asian Woman in BBC Viral Video Was The Nanny?" discusses what unconscious biases might have caused people's wrong assumption about Mrs. Kim being the nanny. "Many people feel the assumption that Mrs. Kim was a helper, rather than the children's mother, was grounded in racial stereotypes about the roles played by Asian women. Another factor that may have led to the assumptions that Mrs. Kim was a nanny is the fact that many still assume, consciously or unconsciously, that people tend to date others from the same ethnic group."[23]

Basically people's fast brain very quickly put Mrs. Kim in a box and assumed she was the nanny. But being Asian is just one of the characteristics that influence people to put others in "boxes." These boxes

[23] CHEUNG, Helier. Why Did People Assume An Asian Woman in BBC Viral Video Was the Nanny? *BBC News*, March 11, 2017. Available at: <https://www.bbc.com/news/world-asia-39244325>. Accessed on: October 10, 2019.

generate what Behavioral Economics calls cognitive shortcuts, the fast "if this, then that," such as "if she is Asian, then she is the nanny."

These boxes, also referred to as stereotypes, exist in our minds and make us come to conclusions about someone else just because they are a woman, man, straight, homosexual, Catholic, Brazilian, Australian, from the North, from the South, black, white, tall or even wearing a t-shirt. All of these features put people in boxes and we quickly come to conclusions about them based on how we built the image of the particular stereotypes in our minds. It is then that the fast brain acts by making these hasty assumptions. We have stereotypes built in our minds that need to be deconstructed so that we can be fairer and our interpretation is closer to reality. "We need to talk about it and deconstruct stereotypes," as Ana Malvestio said in her *Harvard Business Review* article. She talks about fast thinking using the so-called "surgeon riddle."

> *A father and son are in a horrible car crash that kills the dad. The son is rushed to the hospital; just as he's about to go under the knife, the surgeon says: "I can't operate—that boy is my son!" Explain.*

This riddle was posted on Facebook and had over 100,000 shares, 10,000 comments, and 80,000 reactions on *Quebrando o Tabu,* a popular Facebook page in Brazil.

As Ana explained: "When reading the text, it looks like most people are being questioned. How would the boy be the son of the most competent person in the operating room if his father died in the accident? Several theories and hypotheses are raised about the case:

The mother has an extramarital affair? Were they a gay couple? Was the father a foster one? Or anything that might make sense out of the text. What many do not immediately think is that the most competent person in the operating room is the boy's mother, as women are not usually associated with these activities."[24]

The article "The Importance of the Surgeon Riddle: What a Classic Puzzle Reveals About Gender Bias", published on verywellhealth.com, has an interesting take on stereotypes based on the age of who answered the riddle:

> *When* Good Morning America *approached random people on the streets of New York City with this riddle, the great majority could not come up with the right answer. But when the producers asked a group of fifth-graders from a Manhattan school the same riddle, most of the kids got the answer right. And those who didn't get the answer right came up with unique answers, answers none of the grown-ups came up with. For instance, they suggested the surgeon might have been boy's stepfather, or perhaps his 'other dad' on the theory the boy's parents were a gay couple. The kids' answers to the riddle revealed that unlike adults, they had no pre-formed ideas about what kind of person a surgeon should be. They did not assume that the surgeon must be a straight male.*[25]

---

24 MALVESTIO, Ana. A desconstrução do preconceito. Harvard Bussinesse Review, March, 2017. Available at: <https://hbrbr.uol.com.br/desconstrucao-preconceito/>. Accessed on: October 10, 2019.

25 TORREY, Trisha. The Importance of the Surgeon Riddle. *Very Well Health*, August 19, 2019. Available at: <https://www.verywellhealth.com/riddle-me-this-who-is-the-surgeon-3969767>. Accessed on: October 10, 2019.

This is definitely an example of what is defined as gender unconscious bias, i.e., we put someone in a box because she is a woman or because he is a man. Of course, there are people who can quickly and naturally understand that it's the boy's mother, but it is undeniable that women are associated with certain positions, environments, and behaviors for most people, and there are several associations as those that we need to deconstruct.

What does it mean to you when the only information you know about someone is their gender? Have you ever come to the wrong conclusions because you thought with your fast brain and assumed certain things due to someone's gender? What other boxes, beyond gender, do you think influence our decisions and conclusions about people we don't know? Think consciously about stereotypes and always question your assumptions when they are merely based on a few characteristics.

I DON'T THINK, THEREFORE I CLICK

In a digital world where we are tweeting, watching videos, listening to music, and answering emails all at the same time, our attention is divided. We do most of these things with our fast brain, full of problems, stereotypes, boxes, and hasty conclusions—the cognitive shortcuts. It's much more likely to make a mistake in a tweet today, in the digital world, in the midst of a whirlwind of other things we're experiencing, than in the old days when someone used to sit down to write a letter. The distractions around us waste our cognitive processing and our energy. The digital world makes us split our attention, and we do most things with our fast, problematic brain.

Focusing on one thing at a time in the digital world decreases the likelihood of making mistakes and being biased online.

The infographic below, called "An Internet Minute," by @LoriLewis and @OfficiallyChadd, collects the online activity of billions of people globally, in order to see what an internet minute looks like.

Here's what happens on the internet in one minute:

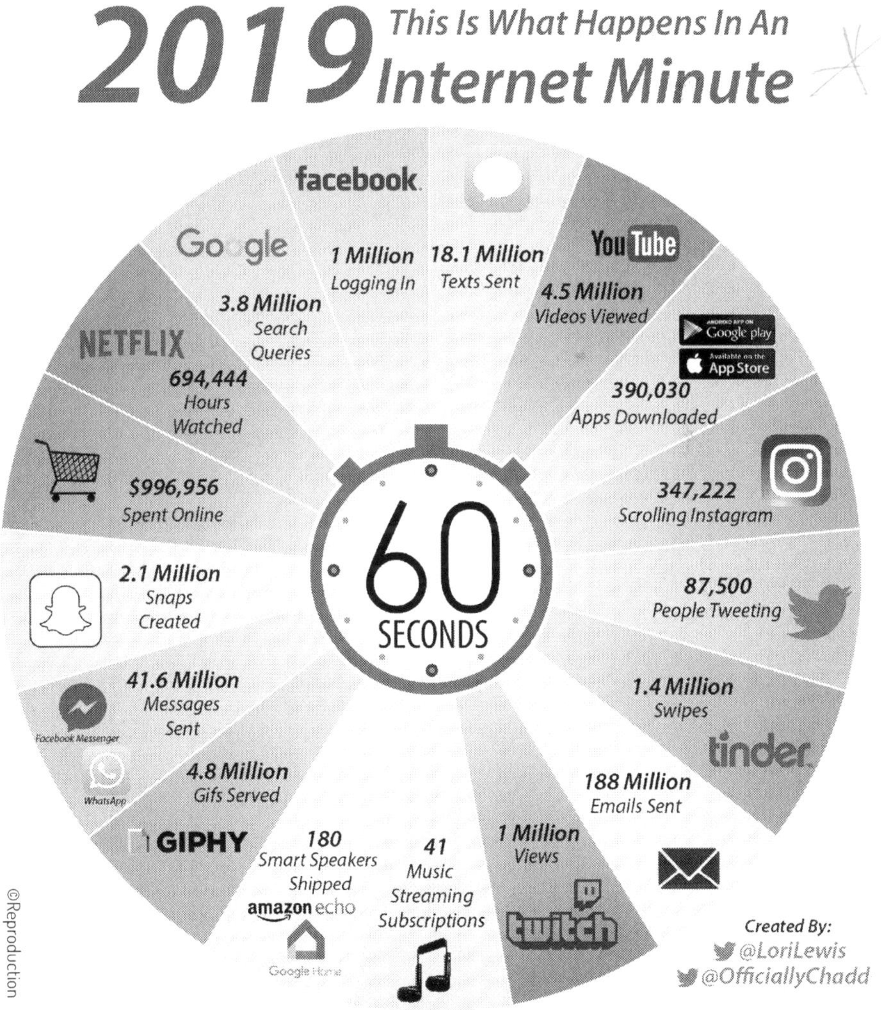

- 41.6 million messages are sent on WhatsApp and Facebook Messenger.
- 188 million emails are sent.
- 1.4 million swipes on Tinder.
- 694,000 hours of video are streamed by Netflix.
- And much more!

Is there time to stop and think before you like, swipe or click? In 2014, Mark Zuckerberg said users were asking for a "dislike" button, but the company wanted to avoid embarrassment among internet users. Embarrassment is just one of the big risks that a possible button with a negative reaction such as "dislike" could cause. Cyberbullying is a type of violence against someone on the internet or other related technologies. It means using virtual space to threaten and annoy someone by slandering, insulting or cowardly attacking.

According to Wikipedia,[26] this type of harassment has become increasingly common in our society, especially among young people. The website *Bullying Statistics* published, among other figures and findings, that "cyberbullying victims are more likely to have low self-esteem and commit suicide." The campaign *"Think before you type—end cyberbullying"*[27] aims to make people aware that they are using their fast-paced, stereotypical brain when they threaten or insult someone online. "Think before," in other words, means: Use your slow brain,

[26] WIKIPEDIA. Virtual Harassment. Available at: <https://en.wikipedia.org/wiki/Cyberbullying>. Accessed on: May 5, 2019.

[27] THINK BEFORE YOU TYPE. Fighting Cyberbullying. Available at: <https://www.thinkbeforeyoutypeinc.org/>. Accessed on: May 5, 2019

FOCUSING ON ONE THING AT A TIME IN THE DIGITAL WORLD DECREASES THE LIKELIHOOD OF MAKING MISTAKES AND BEING BIASED ONLINE.

#DigitalNudge

spend a little more time wondering if that's what you want to type, think about the consequences, beware of your cognitive limitations and know that it can have a very serious negative impact on the person reading on the other side of the screen.

In 2004, psychologist John Suler explained in his article, "The 6 Factors of the Online Disinhibition Effect," which are the factors that fundamentally change the way people interact with each other when online:

1. Anonymity: "My actions cannot be attributed to me."
2. Invisibility: "No one can judge my tone or who I am."
3. Asynchrony: "What I do has no immediate effect."
4. Solipsist introjection: "I'm not seeing anyone, so I have to guess who these people are and their intentions."
5. Dissociative imagination: "The online world is different from the physical world; these people on the other side are not real."
6. Authority minimization: "There is no authority in the online world."

Many people that display hostile attitudes and behaviors online, such as cyberbullies, are not even aware of it. They are interacting using their fast brain; all these effects are influencing their behavior at a level below consciousness, in the case of digital behaviors, below digital consciousness. That's why campaigns like "Think Before You Type" are important; they create a "trigger" that can bring the fast brain to the slow brain, so that people think better about the consequences of their actions.

If you are going to write a negative comment on social media (Facebook, Instagram, WhatsApp) or to anyone digitally, think twice

THE 6 FACTORS OF ONLINE DISINHIBITION EFFECT

BY JOHN SULER

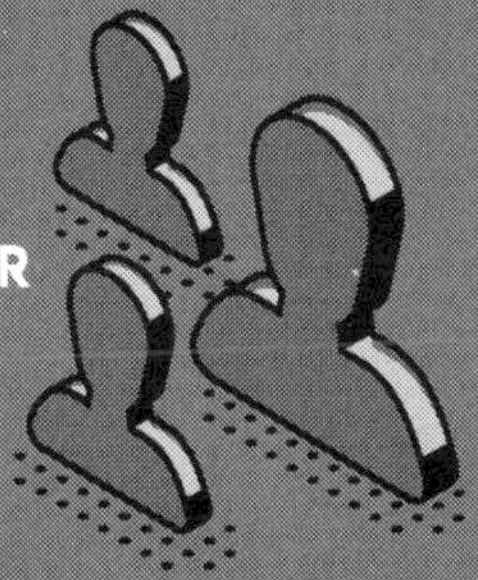

1. **ANONYMITY:** "MY ACTIONS CANNOT BE ATTRIBUTED TO ME".

2. **INVISIBILITY:** "NO ONE CAN JUDGE MY TONE OR WHO I AM".

3. **ASYNCHRONY:** "WHAT I DO HAS NO IMMEDIATE EFFECT".

4. **SOLIPSIST INTROJECTION:** "I'M NOT SEEING ANYONE, SO I HAVE TO GUESS WHO THESE PEOPLE ARE AND THEIR INTENTIONS".

5. **DISSOCIATIVE IMAGINATION:** "THE ONLINE WORLD IS DIFFERENT FROM THE PHYSICAL WORLD; THESE PEOPLE ON THE OTHER SIDE ARE NOT REAL".

6. **AUTHORITY MINIMIZATION:** "THERE IS NO AUTHORITY IN THE ONLINE WORLD".

before writing and sending it. Stop and think for at least ten minutes. Think before you type.

Only in 2016 did Facebook decide to offer other buttons besides "like." These are the so-called "reactions": Love, Ha-ha, Wow, Sad, and Angry. Currently, studies show a great concern over how these reactions could influence online behavior. Note that the slightly negative reactions include "Sad" and "Angry," and yet there is no intention of offending another person, they are just expressions of how the user who is pressing that button feels. Congratulations to Facebook!

After awakening to my consciousness and realizing that I have two brain systems—one fast, one slow—and the online interaction numbers mentioned above, and inspired by the first modern philosopher, René Descartes, who said "I think, therefore I am," I'm sure that, like the 4.3 billion digital citizens, "I don't think, therefore I click". And that's dangerous.

GORILLAS, LIES, AND INVISIBLE EMAILS

Imagine someone asked you to watch a video of six people playing with basketballs. Out of the six subjects, half have white shirts and half have black shirts. Your goal is to pay close attention and count how many times people in white shirts pass the ball to each other.

#DigitalNudge

IF YOU ARE GOING TO WRITE A NEGATIVE COMMENT ON SOCIAL MEDIA (FACEBOOK, INSTAGRAM, WHATSAPP) OR TO ANYONE DIGITALLY, THINK TWICE BEFORE WRITING AND SENDING IT. STOP AND THINK FOR AT LEAST TEN MINUTES. THINK BEFORE YOU TYPE.

You watch the video and eventually are asked if there was anything different about the movie. You answer "no" and correctly confirm the number of passes. Then they ask if there was a gorilla in the video. You get shocked and say: "A gorilla?! Of course not!"

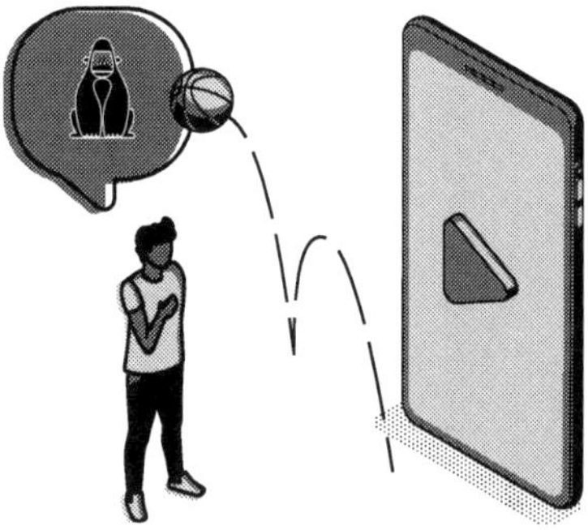

This experiment was proposed by psychologists Daniel Simons and Christopher Chabris. Half of the volunteers did not see the gorilla that appeared in the middle of the video, looked at the camera, thumped his chest, and left. This shocking result reveals that people in general are so focused on one event that they become "blind" to others.

This and other studies prove what is known as Inattentional Blindness, a lack of attention that does not entail vision defects. It happens when an individual fails to perceive an unexpected stimulus because their attention was focused on something else. When there is too much happening around us in a given situation, a temporary "blindness" effect can happen. The term was coined by Arien Mack and Irvin Rock in 1992 and was used as the title of their book. Basically, when you are very focused on a task, it is difficult to notice important things happening around you.

Who has not experienced the classic situation where someone asks: "Did you read that email?" And you think: "Which email? I don't remember receiving it."

I ran an experiment I called Digital Gorilla with hundreds of people. I ask them to answer a three-question form. After everyone has answered the form, I ask if anyone read the text at the beginning. This initial text told participants not to answer question 3 on the form, but most people didn't read it, they just agreed and started answering the form, meaning this text is a gorilla passing invisibly through us. How often and how many times have we accepted terms of conditions without reading them? Juliana Maian says the sentence "I have read and agree to the terms" is the biggest lie in the world.

Hello, let's get started? Thank you for joining us ;-)

35,000. This is the average number of decisions a human being makes every day. It means approximately one decision every two seconds. Of these, have you ever wondered how many are digital decisions, i.e., the ones we make using devices such as smartphones, tablets, computers, wearables etc.? Or the ones that digital devices often make for us? **To show that you are aware of your decisions and you pay attention to everything you read in the digital world, don't answer question 3, just answer questions 1 and 2.** By clicking "Get Started" you agree to join this experiment. Unconscious biases (cognitive biases): Systematic errors regarding how we think and make decisions. Just as in optical illusions we see something different from reality, while making decisions biases influence us to consider a limited reality. Scientists such as Nobel Prize winner Daniel Kahneman have been studying and cataloging these biases for decades so that we can better understand what they call human irrationality.

#DigitalNudge

“I HAVE READ AND AGREE TO THE TERMS” IS THE BIGGEST LIE IN THE WORLD.

JULIANA MAIAN

One further example comes from another experiment I ran when I spoke at a TEDx event. The email approving the registration had the following text:

> One of this year's talks is about default digital decisions. By signing up for this TEDx, you are automatically giving away the power of all the decisions you will make for the rest of your life to the speaker who will talk about decisions. If you don't want to accept this, it's easy, just opt out here at this link.

There were over 400 people registered and only 13 clicked on the opt out link. That was a default decision, a nudge we had made, and participants had to "opt out," but less than 4% did. Not because they wanted me to make all their decisions for them, but because they hadn't read it and the requirement was imposed without them knowing it.

THE 5 DIGITAL CONSCIOUSNESS SKILLS

Ok, let's assume that by now you want to awake and raise your digital consciousness, you want to be more aware of digital nudges and all the hidden forces that influence your behavior when you're in the digital world. How can this happen? What does it mean to have a higher level of digital consciousness? Where to start?

It's not really as simple as pushing a button and simply going from unconscious to conscious. It is a journey. There isn't one group of people who are unconscious and another group of conscious people. Each one of us is going through a process, an awakening of our digital consciousness.

There have been many attempts to define consciousness. One I like is the ability of the mind to perceive the relationship between oneself and its surroundings. According to Max Velmans and Susan Schneider: "Anything that we are aware of at any given moment forms part of our consciousness." In the case of digital consciousness, the "surrounding" is the digital world, the thing we are aware of is our digital interaction with smartphones, tablets, computers, sensors, augmented and virtual

1. **CONTROL OF DIGITAL DECISION**
   "MY DECISIONS, MY RULES"

2. **CONNECTED-DISCONNECTED BALANCE**
   "SOMETIMES WE HAVE TO DISCONNECT IN ORDER TO CONNECT"

3. **KNOWLEDGE OF UNCONSCIOUS BIASES**
   "I SEE BIASES!"

4. **CONCENTRATION AND DIGITAL FOCUS**
   "WHEN WE FOCUS ON EVERYTHING, WE FOCUS ON NOTHING"

5. **CRITICAL THINKING**
   "DOUBT BEFORE BELIEVING, VALIDATE BEFORE SHARING"

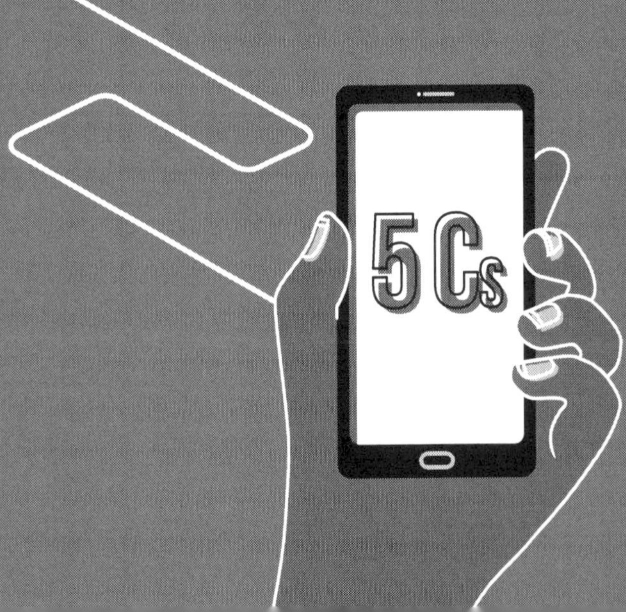

reality, and all the technologies that are and will be part of our lives. We then define digital consciousness as the ability of the mind to perceive the relationship between oneself and the digital world. The ability to perceive this complex environment happens through 5 skills, also known as the 5 Cs of Digital Consciousness.

1. CONTROL OF DIGITAL DECISIONS

"MY DECISIONS, MY RULES"

One of these days, I was booking a hotel room for one of my trips. I went to one of the most famous websites to look for hotels, searched the city and the dates of the trip, and some options were available. I clicked on one of them and when I was looking at the room that interested me the most, red messages started popping up, saying:

- "Hotel in high demand."
- "This is the last room available at this hotel."
- "16 other people are viewing this room right now."
- "Promotional price expires on..." and a countdown, looking like an action movie ticking bomb that would explode if I didn't click on BOOK NOW fast!

A very strong force inside of me was saying: Fabio, just click "Book Now!" before one of those 16 people gets the room. This is the last room in this hotel and demand is high! I stopped, took a deep breath and thought: is this room really the one I want? Are these messages all true or are they digital nudges to influence me to book this as fast as I can without thinking consciously if this is the best decision for me?

Until the day I'm writing this, I still don't know if the messages were true or not, and that's why I think it is best not to name the website. But even if I wasn't sure, I decided not to book that room. I didn't click right away, I thought more consciously and realized that booking for those reasons wouldn't be a decision I'd be making. The control of that digital decision I was about to make was in somebody else's hands. I took a better look at the price and the hotel location, and made my own decision based on my intentions, my reasoning, and my rules, not on the standards that some website or app was trying to push on me. Of course, this information is often true and some digital products will try to influence us in a good way, some will try to use persuasion rather than coercion to influence a decision. The most important thing is to learn how to identify any attempt at influencing you that might be happening and to have control over our decisions.

Science has proven there are countless ways to influence someone to choose, buy, log-in, sign-in, order, submit, accept, search, click or basically make digital decisions. Websites, apps, and all means of digital interactions available use powerful tools to influence people to do things they don't even know they're doing. People buy without knowing what they're buying, give access to their personal data without knowing exactly to whom, click, accept, decide, and then have to bear the consequences of decisions they think they have made consciously and over which they believe they have control, but in fact were heavily influenced, immensely nudged.

People who have the skills to **control digital decisions** can identify when they are being influenced online and make their own decisions.

WHERE TO START AND HOW TO DEVELOP THIS SKILL?

The most important approach to developing control over your digital decisions is to ask yourself what mechanisms a website or application might be using to influence your decision. Studying and delving into these mechanisms will also help, since, if you do not know how you are influenced and manipulated, you will not be able to visualize the strategies and take control.

2. CONNECTED-DISCONNECTED BALANCE

"SOMETIMES WE HAVE TO DISCONNECT IN ORDER TO CONNECT"

In 2018, I took a nine-month sabbatical; it was one of the most amazing experiences of my life. One of the places I visited was Paris and of course I couldn't help but go to the Louvre museum. There I noticed that many people would stop in front of the *Mona Lisa*, take a selfie and leave without even noticing what was right in front of them: One of the world's most well-known and famous paintings, Leonardo da Vinci's most remarkable work. It was right there in front of them and they didn't even look at it. Why? Because the most important thing was to take a selfie and post it on social media to show they were there and saw the *Mona Lisa*. But had they really seen it? Had they been present during that moment? How will they remember it? Would it be the same as searching online for a picture of *Mona Lisa* and looking at it?

I realized that something similar happens several times in our lives and it is important to be disconnected to truly live that moment that happens around us. Not only with a work of art, a sunset, a live concert or a soccer game at a stadium, but also when important people are with us. A family dinner, a friend's birthday, a daily breakfast with someone we love, when instead of asking: "How was your evening? Did you sleep well? What did you dream about last night?," we chose to keep looking at our smartphones—often just scrolling through other people's feeds. In these cases, the digital world, instead of helping us to be more connected, disconnects us from the reality that is right in front of us.

Technology exists to support, engage and connect, but sometimes it disturbs, muddles and disconnects. I travel a lot and while I'm away I try to use video conferencing to communicate with people I love who are far away. I work with people around the world and use technology to connect with them. But when I'm with people in front of me, physically there, I need to disconnect from the digital world in order to connect with the present moment.

This **connected-disconnected balance** is essential to our digital well-being, a term coined by Google in 2018. Android is the core system for over 2 billion users worldwide, and, realizing how important this balance is, Google now offers a functionality in Android 9 that helps us improve our digital wellbeing.

People who have the ability to establish the connected-disconnected balance know how to control their screen time on smartphones and all digital devices, like watching series, scrolling on social media, etc. They know when it is important to be online and when you need to disconnect in order to connect to the offline world.

#DigitalNudge

TECHNOLOGY EXISTS TO SUPPORT, ENGAGE AND CONNECT, BUT SOMETIMES IT DISTURBS, MUDDLES AND DISCONNECTS.

WHERE TO START AND HOW TO DEVELOP THIS SKILL?

The first step is digital self-awareness, understanding your current presence and footprint in the digital world. How long do you spend on your phone or other screens? What apps and websites do you use? Every time you are immersed in the digital world, ask yourself if there is anything going on outside of it that should get more of your attention. When meeting people, prioritize physical interactions, eye-to-eye conversations, over using your smartphone. If someone next to you is connected and this is bothering you for some reason, you can bring a bit of digital awareness to that situation by talking about this skill and the benefits of disconnecting in order to connect.

3. KNOWLEDGE OF UNCONSCIOUS BIASES

"I SEE BIASES!"

Earlier, while explaining the skill of controlling digital decisions, I mentioned my experience booking a hotel, in which the website tried to influence me with some very persuasive messages, do you remember?

Behind each of these messages, lies something very powerful called unconscious biases, which I have mentioned before. Unconscious biases are systematic errors in the way we think and make decisions. When a bias is triggered, we are influenced to make a decision that, without such a trigger, we would not make so often.

Next, I describe the biases that were being used to influence the decision to book the hotel in each of the messages displayed to me:

> Hotel in high demand and 16 other people are now viewing this room:
   - **Bandwagon effect**: The tendency to do (or believe) things because many other people do (or believe) the same. Also related to groupthink and herd behavior.
   - "Since everyone is doing it, I will do it too."

> This is the last room available at this hotel:
   - **Scarcity bias**: When an object or resource is less readily available, due to limited quantity or time, we tend to perceive it as more valuable.
   - "It's running out, it must be good."

> Promotional price expires on:
   - **Loss aversion**: Individuals tend to be more affected by losses than gains.
   - "I cannot afford losing this room!"

There are more than 150 cognitive biases cataloged by behavioral science—I only mentioned three. When I started to study biases, I came to see them everywhere and in every situation—there is even a bias that explains why this happened, the so-called confirmation bias, which is the tendency to search for information that affirms one's beliefs or hypotheses.

These biases happen below your level of consciousness, nudges are interventions to influence you to make, most of the times, an unconscious decision. Having the knowledge of cognitive biases is quite important for both people who are being nudged and people who want to nudge.

People who are able to recognize unconscious biases know and understand the biases and mental triggers that influence decisions in the digital world can identify when one is being used to influence a decision so as not to be fooled or manipulated.

WHERE TO START AND HOW TO DEVELOP THIS SKILL?

The best way to start is to study the cataloged biases and try to identify situations in your daily life where any of them are present. These situations can happen in both the physical and digital worlds, so you will learn about unconscious biases and train your brain to identify them. I'm sure the same thing that happened to me will happen to you! Remember the boy in the movie *The Sixth Sense* that said "I see dead people"? Yeah... "*I see biases*" all the time!

4. CONCENTRATION AND DIGITAL FOCUS

"WHEN WE FOCUS ON EVERYTHING, WE FOCUS ON NOTHING"

Have you ever been focused on reading a book for hours? Ever sat down to play a musical instrument and put all your focus on it? Ever ridden your motorcycle for hours, just concentrated on the road? Books, musical instruments, motorcycles, and others are means to help us exercise two fundamental elements of our mind: concentration and focus. Even when we are not doing one of these activities, it is possible to exercise the ability to focus by observing something that happens to basically every human being all the time: our breath. Focusing on breathing is one of the most common and simple types of meditation, as we are all breathing all the time. But let's not confuse ordinary and simple with easy. It's not easy to reach that level of focus and observe all the thoughts that are popping into our minds as if they were an external entity to who we really are, have you ever tried?

And have you ever tried to pick up your smartphone and focus on one thing for just fifteen minutes? Can you do it? And for an hour? Of course not, because before the first minute there are already three WhatsApp notifications and eight Instagram likes that invade your attention and influence you to click on the notifications to see who is talking to you. It turns out that most of the time these distractions are usually not important; they might be just another meme in the family group text or likes in a photo you didn't even remember posting.

Distractions and more distractions hamper your concentration. What's even worse is that, if we don't get these notifications, it seems that something is wrong and then we check it manually, scrolling the feed, to see if anything happened. We are increasingly drawn to checking if something has happened on our phones. This fear that we feel all the time about not seeing something on social media even has a name, it is called FOMO (Fear of Missing Out). This digital anxiety is characterized by the "desire to remain continually connected to what others are doing." The term FOMO was first mentioned in 2000 by Dan Herman and defined years later by Andrew Przybylski and Patrick McGinnis as the fear that others will have good experiences you won't.

What is remarkable is that this fear is linked to one of the cognitive biases called loss aversion, meaning everything is connected to behavioral science. Fear, the F on FOMO, is one of the most negative things we can ever feel. Feeling fear does not help us progress, or move forward positively in life. Therefore, I am a much bigger fan of JOMO (Joy of Missing Out, or the joy of living here and now without the anxiety of being everywhere at all times). The best description of what JOMO I have ever read is from Kristen Fuller on a *Psychology Today* article:

> "JOMO (the joy of missing out) is the emotionally intelligent antidote to FOMO and is essentially about being present and being content with where you are in life. You do not need to compare your life to others but instead, practice tuning out the background noise of the 'shoulds' and 'wants' and learn to let go of worrying whether you are doing something wrong. JOMO allows us to live life in the slow lane, to appreciate human connections, to be mindful of our time, to practice saying 'no,' to give ourselves 'tech-free breaks,' and to give us permission to acknowledge where we are and to feel emotions, whether they are positive or negative. Instead of constantly trying to keep up with the Jones', JOMO allows us to be who we are in the present moment, which is the secret to finding happiness. When you free up that competitive and anxious space in your brain, you have so much more time, energy and emotion to conquer your true priorities."[28]

[28] FULLER, Kristen. JOMO: The Joy of Missing Out. Psychology Today, July 26, 2018. Available at: <https://www.psychologytoday.com/intl/blog/happiness-is-state-mind/201807/jomo-the-joy-missing-out>. Accessed on: October 10, 2019.

WE ARE HOOKED ON CHECKING IF SOMETHING HAS HAPPENED ON OUR PHONE. WHEN WE FOCUS ON EVERYTHING, WE DON'T FOCUS ON ANYTHING.

#DigitalNudge

On her article, Kristen also mentions the artistic definition of JOMO by Michael Leunig, an Australian cartoonist and poet who was declared an Australian Living Treasure by the National Trust of Australia in 1999:

> *"Oh the joy of missing out.*
> *When the world begins to shout*
> *And rush towards that shining thing;*
> *The latest bit of mental bling–*
> *Trying to have it, see it, do it,*
> *You simply know you won't go through it;*
> *The anxious clamoring and need*
> *This restless hungry thing to feed.*
> *Instead, you feel the loveliness;*
> *The pleasure of your emptiness.*
> *You spurn the treasure on the shelf*
> *In favor of your peaceful self;*
> *Without regret, without a doubt.*
> *Oh the joy of missing out"*
> —Michael Leunig

Let me confess something about myself: for a long time, I tried to focus on things I wanted to do but wasn't able to, as my attention was constantly diverted. It was as if my hand tingled and I wanted to check if messages had arrived on my smartphone or if any of my posts had been liked. While I tried to do thing A, I felt like I could be doing B, C, D and E on my smartphone, laptop or tablet. Although I was sure that I was doing the most important thing then and there, I had a feeling that I should be on another screen or a different app, doing other things. I used to have dozens of tabs open on my laptop, dozens of applications running at the same time and I couldn't focus on anything. Because when we focus on everything, we focus on nothing.

I realized that lack of concentration and focus was killing my productivity. Then I started to use a variety of techniques that helped me focus on exactly what I want and need to do in both the digital and physical worlds. Here I'm going to talk about my journey, from where I started and how I developed my concentration and digital focus skill. This does not mean it works for everyone, but you might get inspired by some of the things I went through on my journey.

We are hooked on checking if something has happened on our phone. When we focus on everything, we don't focus on anything.

WHERE TO START AND HOW TO DEVELOP THIS SKILL?

The first step I took was to do only one thing at a time. One of our biggest enemies while focusing is trying to do several things at once.

Try to ask yourself: "What is the one thing I'm doing right now?" It's important that it has a purpose, a goal, so we have to define that, too.

I use some tools for this, and the one that works best is the Kanban Board. It shows what I need to do, what I am doing and what I have already done (To Do, Doing, Done). In the "Doing" column, there can be only one thing at a time. It's not productive to organize that important presentation, watch a video on YouTube and scroll the Instagram feed at the same time. The board can be physical—with post-its—or digital—a great digital tool is Trello.

A very common situation is when we are doing something and remembering that we have to do something else. Just as I was writing this, I remembered I have to send an email. Instead of stopping what I'm doing and sending the email, I add an item to the "to do" column of my Trello so I don't forget to do it later. There are several similar methods out there to help you focus, this is a simple one that works for me. It might work for you, too.

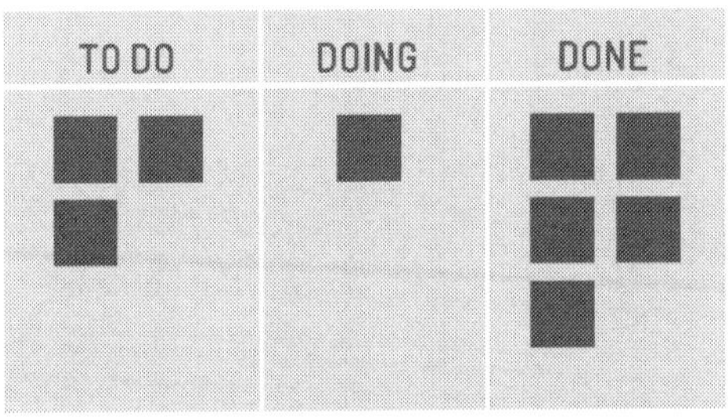

An example of Kanban Board

Another very productive tool I use is the Pomodoro Technique, developed in the late 1980s by an Italian college student who had a brilliant idea. The goal is to increase our productivity and ability to manage time. The technique is applied by creating intense 25-minute concentration flows. Francesco Cirillo, creator of the technique who even wrote a book about it, used a tomato-shaped kitchen timer—hence the name Pomodoro—to focus during those 25 minutes. After that time, is important to take a break for 5 or 10 minutes. This way your brain knows it will have a reward for focusing for 25 minutes. During the

#DigitalNudge

GO THROUGH THE SETTINGS AND DECIDE WHICH APPS HAVE THE POWER TO **DISTRACT** YOU. REMEMBER: IT'S UP TO YOU, NOT THEM OR ME, TO TELL YOU WHAT SHOULD DISTRACT YOU. **YOU** HAVE THE **POWER**!

break, do something unrelated to the goal you were trying to achieve, preferably not in the digital world. Follow the focus-pause cycles.

Of course, the Pomodoro technique is just one way to stayed focus. In general, the important thing is to do one thing at a time and focus on it, thus reducing distractions and minimizing context switching cost. To achieve **concentration and digital focus,** you need to create intense concentration flows with interspersed pauses.

In addition to doing one thing at a time, try to close as many open applications, tabs, and programs as possible so that the open windows don't distract you. Right now, for example, I'm writing this book with only two tabs open: the program I'm writing on and Spotify—because I'm listening to an instrumental playlist for achieving concentration in a way no outside distractions can make me deviate from the book.

Turn off just about all notifications on your digital devices. Go through the settings and decide which apps have the power to distract you. Remember: It's up to you, not them or me to tell you what should distract you. You have the power! In WhatsApp, specifically, I suggest silencing all your groups and most people who are less relevant to you. Leave notifications enabled only for people you want to give the power to distract you.

Nir Eyal is an expert on how to form habits and get people hooked on digital products. His two books, *Hooked* and *Indistractable*, are absolutely phenomenal. One aspect of distractions and habits that Nir talks a lot about are the triggers. Triggers can be internal or external and, according to him, it's important for us to "hack back" these triggers in order for us to be indistractable. I see a huge alignment between being indistractable, which, I agree with Nir, is "the skill of the century", and the concentration and digital focus we are talking about here. In order to be more digitally conscious, I strongly recommend also being indistractable.

People who have **concentration and digital focus** can achieve their goals by using digital devices to their advantage.

5. CRITICAL THINKING

"DOUBT BEFORE BELIEVING, VALIDATE BEFORE SHARING"

If I go to Google and search for the word "digital," what do you think the recommended autocomplete results will be? There are two very different lists that appear:

1. If I have my personal Google Account.
2. If I'm in Google anonymous mode—known as incognito.

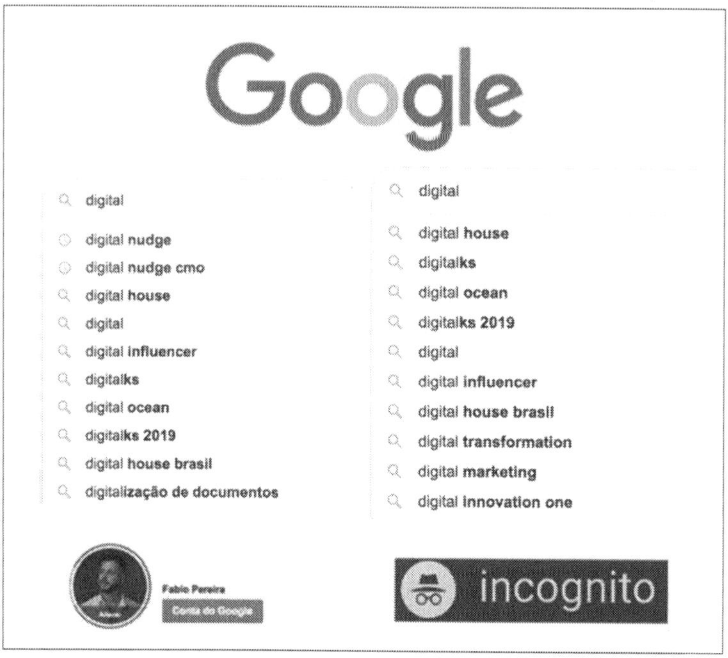

©Reproduction

Why are the results different? Because the internet is not neutral. If you look for the same word, it is very likely that another list of suggestions will come up. When searching for objective things like converting 10 kilograms to pounds, for example, of course the answer will be the same regardless of who is doing the search. But if we use the internet to build an opinion about something (political subjects or other subjective topics that can be interpreted in various ways), it will not be impartial. We trust Google as the absolute truth about many things. You know that famous bar or restaurant table conversation when suddenly someone questions a story or fact and very quickly picks up their smartphone to check it on Google and prove they are right? I've been through this several times! For subjective topics, it can lead to even more conflict if one person finds a result and another one finds something different.

In addition to the digital partiality and the fact that, depending on who is doing the search and where it is being done, the result is different, there is also false information spread on the Internet across multiple channels, which is even worse. These are the famous fake news.

The problem is even more serious because news, information, and data are passed from one person to another across multiple channels—depending on where you are from, one of the most common being WhatsApp today—and many people still believe in everything they read online, thinking: "If it's on the internet, it must be true."

Throughout my journey raising my digital consciousness, I always keep an eye out when people send me something, especially on group texts. Often, I've tried to validate if the information was true and found out it wasn't. What should we do in a situation like that? Depending on the group, I reveal the fact that the information is not true; I believe this helps raise the digital consciousness of my friends from my groups. It is important to explain my validation process and how I found it to be fake news. Sometimes people like it because they learned something new or they learned how to validate if something is true or not. Unfortunately sometimes people feel embarrassed to have shared something that wasn't true, but they also learn from it and improve their critical thinking skill, something that will make them think twice with their slow brain next time if they should even share something before validating.

Guido Lemos and his research team at the Federal University of Paraíba ran a scientific experiment to learn more about the process of creating and spreading fake news. Researchers created some news about a Russian fortune teller who had predicted that Brazil would be the champion of the 2018 Soccer World Cup. The news was spread to over 250,000 people. Guido talked about the experiment at his TEDx talk[29] and I was very glad to be his speaking coach. We worked together on creating the talk and I really like a sentence we created together to summarize how we should act on the topic: *doubt before believing, validate before sharing!* When you share something, your word and your credibility are also being shared.

[29] Available at: <www.youtube.com/watch?v=bC7edeMKWTE>. Accessed on: May 6, 2019.

WHERE TO START AND HOW TO DEVELOP THIS SKILL?

The first step is exactly the key statement we quoted before: Always doubt before believing and always validate before sharing. It is important to be aware that absolutely everything on the internet may not be true, and it is good to have some reliable sources of information, some websites we rely on to search for information and verify its accuracy.

Therefore, the next step is to create a list of websites you trust, credible news portals to check whether something is true or not. It is also important to know about websites whose focus is exactly to find fake news and publishing if that particular news is true or fake. I recommend that you create your own list. The main tip is, and I will repeat it: Always doubt before believing, always validate before sharing.

People who have the skill of **critical thinking** have the capacity to differentiate what is true and false on the internet; they do not spread fake news and know exactly how and where to look for the truth.

Access the references used in this chapter scanning this QR code!

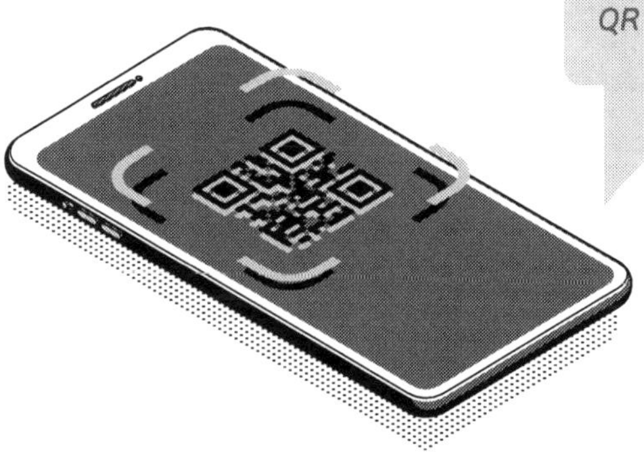

DOUBT BEFORE BELIEVING, VALIDATE BEFORE SHARING!

#DigitalNudge

ARTIFICIAL INTELLIGENCE BIAS

WHITE MASKS, CLOSED EYES, AND DIGITAL BIAS

Imagine a child who has an apple in his or her hand, and an adult says: "Apple!" Soon after, the child repeats: "Apple" and of course it will sometimes sound like "ap-up" or "ap-oh", but after a few tries they will learn that it is an apple. After a few days, the child sees an apple and, without any adult saying anything, he or she will point to it and say: "Apple!" The child has gone through two stages—training and inference, in very simple terms:

1. **Training** is when someone learns what something is.
2. **Inference** is when someone recognizes something based on what they have learned.

We always go through these two stages in our lives. Always learning and inferring, and learning again and inferring again.

A few weeks later the same child sees a green apple and does not say "apple." Why? Because when they were trained to learn what an apple was, the green apple was not part of the training. Now the child doesn't know what fruit that is. Although there is a similarity, the color is different; sometimes the size is also different. What now? They will have to be retrained to broaden their knowledge of the world and learn that a green apple is also an apple.

With computers and digital devices there is a similar process of training and inference. There is something called deep learning that very well defines these two stages of training and inference.

The image below, inspired by one of Nvidia's blog,[30] explains the difference between these two phases very well with an example of training using photos of cats.

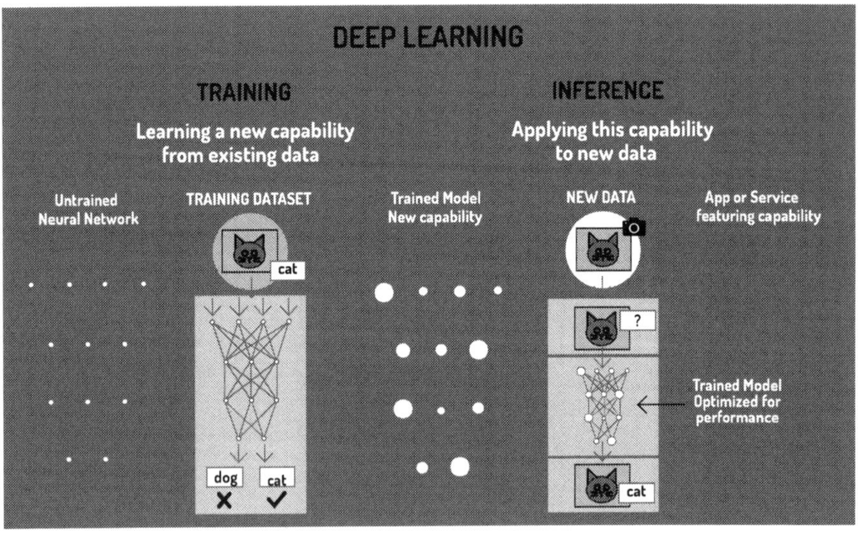

Your phone can categorize all the photos you have taken and whether they are photos of apples or not. In fact, this process is far more advanced than that! Today's computers can categorize photos

30 Available at: <www.blogs.nvidia.com/blog/2016/08/22/difference-deep-learning-training-inference-ai>. Accessed on: May 6, 2019.

and know who is in them through a technology called facial recognition. You can take photos of dozens of people, and Google Photos, Facebook, and other face recognition software group together photos of similar people and even know who they are.

The first step in this process is to identify that in a photo there is a person and not an apple, for instance. Computers are "trained" to do this with examples of people and apples:

- Photos of people: "Hey computer, these are photos of people."
- Photos of apples: "Hey computer, these are photos of apples."

As we saw above, in Artificial Intelligence this step is also called training. Now imagine that you have downloaded one of these face recognition apps because you want to categorize your friends and family in the photos on your smartphone and realize that the app never recognizes you in any of the photos you have.

You run some tests, take photos of various friends and discover that the application does recognize the faces of some people and not others. Yours is one of the faces that are never recognized. The app simply does not know that you are a person. Joy Buolamwini is an MIT student who went through a similar situation when she discovered that face recognition system did not recognize her face but did recognize that of other people. It got worse when she discovered that the system did not recognize the dark-skinned faces of black people because, when the software went through the "training" process, people who were training it did not think to use pictures of black people and say: "Hey computer, this is a face."

That's the kind of problem Joy has been discussing and researching in her InCoding project (inclusive coding).[31] Joy wore a white mask for a while to raise awareness of the fact that the software would only recognize her face with the mask on. That is, the software recognizes a mask as a real face, but does not recognize a real face as a face. As nonsensical as it might sound, this is Artificial Intelligence Bias, or AI Bias.

AI bias is what happens when AI systems, computers, algorithms, Artificial Intelligence, robots or any intelligent technology come to wrong conclusions that differ from reality because they have been trained and learned from biased data and from biased people. AI systems only eat what we feed them and they eat data. "Artificial intelligence can actually reinforce bias and exclusion, even when it's used in the most well-intended

[31] JOY BUOLAMWINI. How I'm Fighting Bias in Algorithms. Available in: <https://www.ted.com/talks/joy_buolamwini_how_i_m_fighting_bias_in_algorithms>. Accessed on: May 6, 2019

ways. AI systems are shaped by the priorities and prejudices—conscious and unconscious—of the people who design them," Joy wrote in her *New York Times* article titled "When the Robot Doesn't See Dark Skin".[32] Joy also mentions that research has shown that automated systems that are used to inform several types of decisions are biased.

But technology is not to blame. The accountability lies on the hands of technology leaders who lack digital consciousness, diversity, and inclusion in their data strategies. Data is the information from which Artificial Intelligence learns. Inclusion and diversity are very important dimensions in the AI system training process.

Another example of AI bias happened when Richard Lee, of Asian descent, tried to renew his passport in New Zealand using a very modern robot that recognizes faces. The robot said Richard's photo could not be accepted because "subject eyes are closed."[33]

Remember: Unless you consciously include, you will unconsciously exclude.

Richard said he was not upset because such technology "is relatively new and unsophisticated." The problem here is not sophistication, though, but a lack of awareness and diversity in training data. It lacks a broader and inclusive view when dealing with this type of technology.

A New Zealand government spokesperson said "up to 20 percent of passport photos submitted online are rejected for various reasons."

[32] BUOLAMWINI, Joy. When the Robot Doesn't See Dark Sin. The New York Times, July 21, 2018. Avaliable at: <https://www.nytimes.com/2018/06/21/opinion/facial-analysis-technology-bias.html>. Accessed on: October 10, 2019.

[33] New Zealand Passport Robot Tells Applicant of Asian Descent to Open Eyes. Reuters, December 7, 2016. Available at: <https://www.reuters.com/article/us-newzealand-passport-error/new-zealand-passport-robot-tells-applicant-of-asian-descent-to-open-eyes-iduskbn13w0rl>. Accessed on: May 6, 2019.

#DigitalNudge

REMEMBER: UNLESS YOU CONSCIOUSLY INCLUDE, YOU WILL UNCONSCIOUSLY EXCLUDE.

Fortunately, Richard has had his passport renewed without any problems, but how many other people were not so lucky? This example was reported in more detail in the article "New Zealand Passport Robot Tells Applicant of Asian Descent to Open Eyes." This is a simple case of passport renewal, but what if a citizen does not have access to a hospital, for example, because a biased technology thinks that person is not a person?

Basically, the technology that does not recognize the face of black people or thinks that a user of Asian descent has their eyes closed is biased AI.

THE IRRATIONAL AND BIASED DIGITAL JUDGE

In November 2016, an article was published by the Daily Mail entitled "Do YOU have the 'Face of A Criminal'"? Controversial AI Judges Whether You Are A Crook Based on Facial Features." Obviously, my attention was quickly captured and I was curious to read it. Researchers at Shanghai Jiao Tong University conducted a study to determine whether artificial intelligence can identify if people are criminals or not just by their physical traits. In other words, an AI system was trained with photos of people who were judged and found guilty or innocent. Let's call this system a "digital judge." The digital judge underwent an AI training process and learned about faces of guilty people and what the ones from innocent people look like. For the digital judge, "people with smaller mouths, curvier upper lips and closer-set eyes are more likely to be criminals." To reach these conclusions, the system examined 1.856 faces of men aged 18 e 55 years; 730 of the photos belonged to criminals—although the images were not mugshots.

The statement that shocked me the most in the article was: "Unlike a human examiner/judge, a computer vision algorithm or classifier has absolutely no subjective baggage, having no emotions, no biases whatsoever due to past experience, race, religion, political doctrine, gender, age etc., no mental fatigue, no preconditioning of a bad sleep or meal.[34]" How can it say that this system has no bias? Of course it does! Its decisions are completely based on how it was trained and training data carries biases.

Furthermore, what defines whether someone is guilty or innocent has absolutely nothing to do with their face; being guilty or innocent is related to their behavior and not whether their mouth is small or large. Creating this relationship between the two dimensions, face and the person being guilty or innocent, has already made this digital judge biased since the beginning. Its definition of intelligence is biased because it interprets reality by considering traits that ignore the factor that is mostly needed in order to determine whether someone is guilty or innocent: the behavior and actions of an individual.

DATA DIVERSITY AND INCLUSION AS AN ANTIDOTE TO AI BIAS

Two things are needed in order to reduce the risks and impact of AI bias. First, we have to accept it exists due to the fact that humans are biased and humans create technology. Second, intentional data diversity and inclusion are also essential requirements during the AI training process.

34 BEST, Shivali. Do YOU Have The Face of A Criminal? Controversial AI Judges Whether You Are a Crook Based on Facial Features. Daily Mail, November 21, 2016. Available at: <https://www.dailymail.co.uk/sciencetech/article-3956826/Do-face-criminal-Controversial-AI-judges-law-abiding-based-look-like.html>. Accessed on: October 10, 2019.

BASICALLY, THE TECHNOLOGY THAT DOES NOT RECOGNIZE THE FACE OF BLACK PEOPLE OR THINKS THAT A USER OF ASIAN DESCENT HAS THEIR EYES CLOSED IS **BIASED AI.**

#DigitalNudge

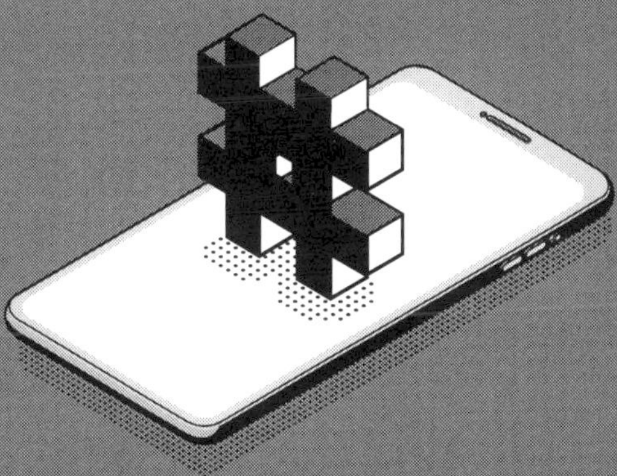

WE MUST ALWAYS ASK: IS THERE ANY DIMENSION THAT WE ARE NOT CONSIDERING THAT CAN GENERATE AI BIAS?

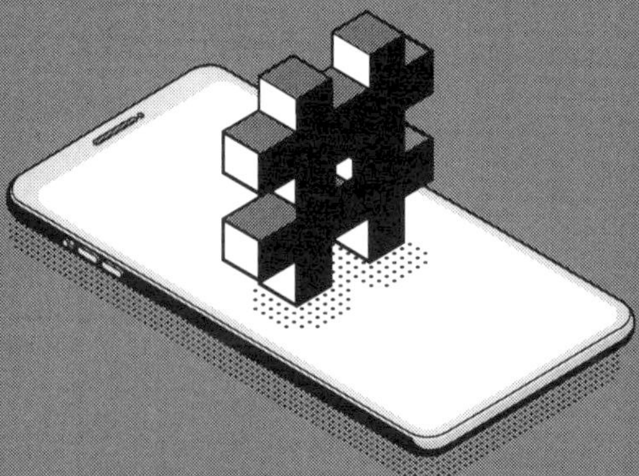

Thinking intentionally about all the dimensions that our fast brain will not reach due to its limitations. Also, deliberately thinking with our slow brain will highlight blindspots. During the training process, we must always ask: Is there any dimension that we are not considering which can generate AI bias? What might happen if we include or exclude certain data dimension?

It is important to remember that algorithms and AI systems will always influence and make digital decisions using the data we give them. We constantly feed computers, smartphones, and apps with data. But the responsibility for that data is far greater for the people in charge of the training phase of algorithms and decision-making systems. This stage, as we saw earlier, is one where AI systems learn how to make a decision. People who feed data systems at this stage need digital consciousness to choose content, and should consider all possible dimensions, including diversity as essential to decreasing the chances of biased digital decisions.

One of the things this book brings you is the "AI bias antidote checklist", which can be accessed by the QR code below. Feel free to share it with someone you might know who needs to be more aware of the risks of AI bias.

TO OFFLOAD OR TO CLUTTER OUR MINDS?

YOU ARE NOT YOUR MIND

Philosopher Descartes believed that he had found the most fundamental truth when he made his famous statement: 'I think, therefore I am.' He had, in fact, given expression to the most basic error: to equate thinking with Being and identity with thinking. The compulsive thinker, which means almost everyone, lives in a state of apparent separateness, in an insanely complex world of continuous problems and conflict, a world that reflects the ever-increasing fragmentation of the mind. The mind is using you. You are unconsciously identified with it, so you don't even know that you are its slave. It's almost as if you were possessed without knowing it, and so you take the possessing entity to be yourself. The beginning of freedom is the realization that you are not the possessing entity—the thinker. Knowing this enables you to observe the entity. The moment you start watching the thinker, a higher level of consciousness becomes activated. You then begin to realize that there is a vast realm of intelligence beyond thought, that thought is only a tiny aspect of that intelligence. You also realize that all the things that truly matter—beauty, love, creativity, joy, inner peace—arise from beyond the mind. You begin to awaken.

This is a quote from Eckhart Tolle's *The Power of Now*, which for the past twenty years has been transforming lives and has sold over 12 million copies and has been published in 35 languages worldwide.[35] One of its most striking quotes is the title of chapter one: "You are not your mind." When I first read it, I began a transformation within myself about who I truly am and who I think I am. We are not our mind. Being and thinking are two distinct entities. According to Eckhart, being is something that exists beyond thinking.

I spent a weekend that has transformed my life at a spiritual retreat with Eckhart Tolle and asked him how he saw the connection between technology and the power of now; I wanted to know if there was a way to use technology to increase humanity's awareness and presence. After thinking for a few seconds, something he always does and which, almost like magic, makes everyone around him more present, he replied in a very conscious way. Among many awakening things that Eckart told me, one of the most impactful ones was: "Smartphones are an extension of our minds" and he spoke about the fact that technology can be used to increase our consciousness or the other way around.

Eckhart also brought to my attention the fact that the human mind is addictive, something we cannot control. Thus, with smartphones

[35] Data from a 2014 article available at: <https://www.christophertitmussblog.org/eckhart-tolle-is-on-the-rich-mans-list-is-this-the-price-of-enlightenment>. Accessed on: May 15, 2019.

"SMARTPHONES ARE AN 'EXTENSION OF OUR MIND'."

ECKHART TOLLE

and digital devices being an "extension of our mind," we need to be aware of the risks posed by our lack of control over how we use them. There are ways to use digital devices to either raise our consciousness or clutter our minds. Technology can also be used to drive humans completely insane, a risk for us to be aware of, according to Eckart.

We ended up having a 16 minute conversation which was recorded, and the video got uploaded to Eckart's YouTube channel with the title of "Consciousness & Technology".[36] Up to this point, it has had over 75,000 views.

TECHNOLOGY CAN BE USED TO OFFLOAD OUR MIND

We wake up thinking about many things: What time do I have to get to work? Am I late? Is that bill due today? How many emails do I have to read? What about that meeting this afternoon? And the bad grade my son got at school? Tonight, I'll go to the supermarket, I cannot forget to buy sweet potatoes. I have to answer that email from my manager.

All these thoughts are cluttering our minds and consuming our attention, which is already limited. What if we had diabetes, like Isabella from Quin, who spends all day "calculating, monitoring, analyzing, remembering, waiting, and worrying about the impact every meal, every activity and every emotion will have on her body"? When

36 Available at: <https://www.youtube.com/watch?v=6k812V97Tz4>. Accessed on: October 10, 2019.

we spoke about Isabella on a previous chapter, she also said that for many years she always dreamed of offloading all this mental effort into a machine.

Have you noticed that she used the term "offload"? That's right! When we think, we are spending a limited resource and it is tiring, it is as if we were carrying such a "load", so our mind gets tired. Quin is just one example of the digital world offloading our mind as it makes decisions for us. Quin's goal is to make as many decisions as possible so you don't have to worry about them or think about when and how to act, no matter where you are and what you're doing. That is, an app to think and act for you, to reduce the burden of worrying. This way, by thinking less, we will be more conscious of who we really are, more aware of our most real self.

As I said earlier, I use two applications for meditation (Headspace and 1 Giant Mind). Meditation is one of the ways to be more aware of who we really are, of our deepest self that goes beyond thinking.

Quin, Headspace, and 1 Giant Mind are just some of the amazing digital products that help us raise our consciousness, which deep down helps us.

Here are a few other examples of how technology has already helped us and can further help offload our minds.

TECHNOLOGY OFFLOADING DRIVERS MINDS

Today, car drivers no longer have to wonder, as they did up to a few years ago, whether they are taking the right path, where to turn right or left or how bad the traffic is at this hour in that busy area of the city. All this information is being processed by technologies like Waze and Google Maps, which simply guide the car by following simple instructions like "turn right 1 mile ahead." Self-driving cars, also known as autonomous cars, which already exist today, will be part of our daily lives in the near future and allow us to simply get in a car and have it take us wherever we want to go. GPS and autonomous cars are technologies that offload drivers' minds.

TECHNOLOGY OFFLOADING PATIENTS MINDS

Did you know that the first virus was discovered in 1892? That's right; it was only over a century ago that we were made aware of viruses. Can you imagine that the virus had always been there, but we did not know of its existence? In other words, people had viral diseases, and no doctor could diagnose it. Today there is technology that can diagnose diseases, sometimes better and more accurately than human doctors do. Medicalfuturist.com has listed 5 ways medical virtual reality is already changing healthcare. Here are two of them:

- Helping patients relax and reduce the stress of being in a hospital by taking them to virtual environments such as beautiful landscapes in Iceland or swimming with whales in the ocean.
- Helping children in treatment feel at home at special events, such as their birthday. It is much better to feel at home wearing virtual reality glasses (VR) than to spend a birthday in a hospital.

In the near future, computers will quickly diagnose diseases and customized treatments will be available to patients. Predictions say that to get a "self-diagnose, we will just spit on our smartphones." Is it an overstatement? Imagine that it will be possible to have sensors integrated into our smartphones and through our saliva they will be able to identify diseases and point out treatments. Do you have a sore throat? Spit on your iPhone and it will tell you what you have, automatically communicating with the nearest pharmacy, which will deliver your medicine via drone to your door in a matter of minutes.

Virtual Reality is a technology that offloads patients' minds.

TECHNOLOGY OFFLOADING SHOPPERS' MINDS

In the old days, when we used to going to the supermarket, we wondered what we needed to buy. Unless we had written a shopping list on paper, we would have to remember everything. Today there are apps that help us maintain lists and even suggest purchases based on what we bought in the past. In the near future, our smart refrigerators will communicate with items inside it and automatically place orders at your favorite grocery store, as everything will be connected to the revolutionary "Internet of Things" (*IoT*).

In 2019 there are over 16 billion things connected to the internet—more than three times the number of internet users, which is 4.3 billion. Amazon patented a product shipping method in 2014 that ships the item even before you actually make a purchase. It is called anticipatory shipping. The method predicts that you are likely to buy

#DigitalNudge

IN 2019 THERE ARE OVER 16 BILLION THINGS CONNECTED TO THE INTERNET— MORE THAN THREE TIMES THE NUMBER OF INTERNET USERS, WHICH IS 4.3 BILLION.

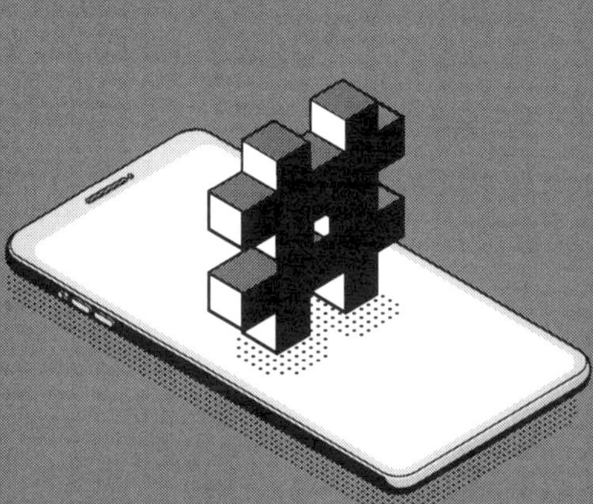

something and Amazon can ship it to you. Have you ever thought about receiving an item you really wanted to buy but haven't purchased yet? That's just about what the company wants to do. The article "Amazon Patents 'Anticipatory' Shipping—To Start Sending Stuff Before You've Bought It" published in *TechCrunch* explains it in more detail. Will we not have to worry about what to buy in the future? Will items appear when needed?

It all sounds very revolutionary, doesn't it? The World Economic Forum, which brings together leading business and political leaders, as well as selected intellectuals and journalists to discuss the most pressing issues facing the world, has defined this transformation as "a technological revolution that will fundamentally change the way we live, work and relate to each other. At its scale, scope, and complexity, the transformation will be different from anything humans have experienced before," says Klaus Schwab, author of *The Fourth Industrial Revolution*.

INVASION OF ATTENTION AND A CONTENT DIET

One of these days, I was tapping and swiping through my Instagram stories—by the way, have you noticed that every social media now has stories? The first app to implement it was Snapchat. You posted a video or a photo and 24 hours later, it disappeared. Facebook tried to buy Snapchat, but no deal was achieved. So, Facebook decided to launch the same feature in all its products. Now there are stories in all social media: Instagram, Facebook, and even WhatsApp, where they're called Status. Very little people post anything, and when you go online to check there are only a few people you didn't even remember you had on your WhatsApp contacts.

But back to the day I was going through my Stories, there was Marcio Paulo, a friend who proposed to his girlfriend. Right after that, I saw my brother Paulo Neto, who is a flight attendant, on one of his flights, this time he was traveling with his boyfriend. When I tap the next story, who did I see? A very famous singer! I thought to myself, "I don't follow her on Instagram, did anyone I follow know her and posted a story with her?" It took a few seconds for me to realize that it was a sponsored story in disguise within mine. I felt invaded, like they were stealing something from me. At that time, I wasn't sure what it was, but then I thought better, I used my slow brain, which needs a little more time to process things, and came to the conclusion that they were stealing one of the most valuable things we have today: our attention. I call it "invasion of attention," a term similar to invasion of privacy, but instead of our privacy being invaded, it is our attention that is literally stolen, and ironically, while we are not even aware. Digital conscious people know when they are experiencing invasion of attention, so they don't let it happen.

We talked at the beginning of this book about how much we are constantly flooded with information. In this new digital age, it is important to decide what we will consume. That's right, it's like we need to be on a digital content diet.

Imagine you have realized that we live in a world full of junk food: Fries, hamburgers, fried chicken, sugar, and more sugar, all available

IN THIS NEW DIGITAL AGE, IT IS IMPORTANT TO DECIDE WHAT WE WILL **CONSUME.** THAT'S RIGHT, IT'S LIKE WE NEED TO BE ON A **DIGITAL CONTENT DIET.**

#DigitalNudge

around every corner. So, you decide to go to a nutritionist to know what you should and should not eat. On Monday morning, you begin the diet and the list contains:

> Breakfast: omelet and avocado (by the way, I love this breakfast).

You wake up pretty excited to eat your breakfast and when you take the second bite, fries with ketchup pop up inside the omelet! You decided to eat something healthy and someone other than you decided to add fries into the filling. How would you feel about that?

Yeah, content delivery platforms like YouTube, for example, now have promotional content in the middle of the videos. Just when we got used to skipping ads within five seconds; my finger itches to press the "skip this ad in 3... 2... 1...." Now, in the middle of the video, sponsored content appears. Have you decided to watch that content? This is an invasion of attention. Here's a walkthrough of how it works:

> You start watching the video you want.
> You "give" your attention to the main video.
> The digital product now has your attention, which is one of the most valuable things we have today.
> In the middle of the video I wanted to watch, a promotional video pops up.

It is at a time of attention vulnerability, when you gave your full attention to the video you wanted to watch, that YouTube captures your attention, showing other promotional content for which they are charging their clients. Yes, the platform BASICALLY sells your attention and makes you eat those fries with ketchup when you were eating an omelet. What do we usually do? We watch the promotional video, not even knowing why it appeared, and THEN continue with the main content.

When you consume free content, your attention is the product someone else is selling. Today there is the so-called attention economy, very well explained by Herbert Simon:

> *The Attention Economy:*
> *... In an information-rich world, the wealth of information means a dearth of something else: a scarcity of whatever it is that information consumes. What information consumes is rather obvious it consumes the attention of its recipients. Hence a wealth of information creates a poverty of attention and a need to allocate that attention efficiently among the overabundance of information sources that might consume it.*[37]

We need to be very careful of who is making money from selling our attention and to whom we are giving that attention, because it is very valuable. Whenever you watch a video on YouTube, you are giving someone money. Yes, you are! Your attention is worth money and, most importantly, it is limited. Learn how to use it well.

We are giving away our most valuable assets—our attention and our data—without understanding the consequences. These assets

[37] Available at: <https://www.goodreads.com/quotes/8502027-in-an-information-rich-world-the-wealth-of-information-means-a>. Accessed on: October 10, 2019.

#DigitalNudge

WE ARE GIVING AWAY OUR MOST VALUABLE ASSETS—OUR ATTENTION AND OUR DATA—WITHOUT UNDERSTANDING THE CONSEQUENCES

are so valuable that Facebook made a profit of over $22 billion dollars in 2018—with over $55 billion dollars of revenue.[38]

There are global movements to raise awareness to how important and valuable our attention is. One of the most popular ones used to be called Time Well Spent, started by Tristan Harris. It is like the organic food movement, but for the Internet. The movement has been renamed to *HumaneTech*[39] and its strategy is based on three steps:

1. Understand the problem.
2. Define the way forward.
3. Their work: Initiatives to address the problems.

As the HumaneTech website defines itself: "This is a historic moment—never before has technology had the power to so profoundly change the beings that create it. We are at a turning point where we can either allow that power to continue unchecked, or contain it by building Humane Technology that protects our minds and replenishes society. Humane Technology requires that we understand our most vulnerable human instincts so we can design compassionately to protect them from abuse."

One of the most valuable jobs in the near future will be digital content nutritionist, a job that can also be called content curation. The job can be carried out automatically by computers that learn from our content consumer habits.

Have you ever thought about not having to read the emails you don't want and not having to watch the ads that don't interest you,

[38] Available at: <https://www.statista.com/statistics/277229/facebooks-annual-revenue-and-net-income>. Accessed on: October 10, 2019.

[39] Learn more at: <http://humanetech.com>. Accessed on: May 15, 2019.

meaning just consuming what you really want and need? It doesn't hurt to dream... Oh, but it does, because when we dream we are investing our attention in the dream, and it is worth a lot! Even so, it is a very valuable investment. Dreaming is worth it!

It is important to make a conscious decision about what content and information we will consume. This is even more important than deciding what to eat. Choose what you read, watch, see, and listen to online.

TURNED OFF SMARTPHONES DRAIN OUR INTELLIGENCE

A 2017 study by *Science of Learning* talks about the cognitive cost of having the "mere presence" of a smartphone nearby, even if it is turned off. The hypothesis researchers wanted to prove was: "Could smartphones influence our cognitive performance, even when they're turned off, but close to us?" Speaking in a simple language, this cognitive performance means two things:

> Ability to process and maintain information (working memory capacity): Consuming some information, such as reading, for example, processing, understanding, and remembering it later. It is a very important ability to understand what we read so that we can explain it later.

> Fluid intelligence: The ability to reason and solve new problems.

Putting it in very simple terms: Does having a smartphone turned off near us make us less intelligent? The answer is yes! Experiment

#DigitalNudge

ONE OF THE MOST VALUABLE JOBS IN THE NEAR FUTURE WILL BE DIGITAL CONTENT NUTRITIONIST, A JOB THAT CAN ALSO BE CALLED CONTENT CURATING.

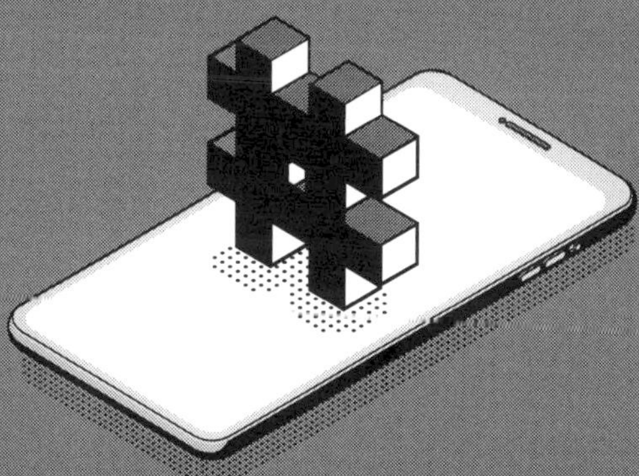

participants who had their turned off smartphones nearby performed worse than participants who left their phones in another room. This means that if we are to solve a difficult problem, we need to focus and use our cognitive processing ability in a more committed way. Smartphones drain our attention, even when turned off, because we keep thinking: "Has someone texted me? Has someone liked my photo on Instagram?" These anxious questions, even if unconscious, drain our brains and our intelligence.

When you need to solve a difficult problem that requires a lot of your attention and intelligence, leave your smartphone in another room and you will see how much easier it is to solve it.

Shlomo Benartzi, in his book *The Smarter Screen,* mentions a study that discovered that worrying about an unread email can lower our IQ by as much as 10 points—the equivalent to missing a whole night's sleep and more than double the 4-point decrease seen after smoking marijuana.[40]

Right now, for example, I'm writing this book in the living room and my smartphone is in my bedroom in airplane mode so I can focus and pay full attention to what I'm doing.

Can you keep your smartphone away for one day? My girlfriend once forgot hers at her mother's house, so she didn't have it for an entire day. Then she told me she wasn't worried about whether someone had texted her and that she had more quality time with me because she didn't have her phone with her. In fact, sometimes when we go to the theater or to the movies, she doesn't bring the device because she

[40] CCN. Emails 'hurt IQ more than pot', 2005. Available at: <http://edition.cnn.com/2005/WORLD/europe/04/22/text.iq/>. Accessed on: October 10, 2019.

#DigitalNudge

IT IS IMPORTANT TO MAKE A CONSCIOUS DECISION ABOUT WHAT CONTENT AND INFORMATION WE WILL CONSUME. THIS IS EVEN MORE IMPORTANT THAN DECIDING WHAT TO EAT. **CHOOSE** WHAT YOU **READ, WATCH, SEE, AND LISTEN TO ONLINE.**

#DigitalNudge

WHEN YOU NEED TO SOLVE A DIFFICULT PROBLEM THAT REQUIRES A LOT OF YOUR ATTENTION AND INTELLIGENCE, LEAVE YOUR SMARTPHONE IN ANOTHER ROOM AND YOU WILL SEE HOW MUCH EASIER IT IS TO SOLVE IT.

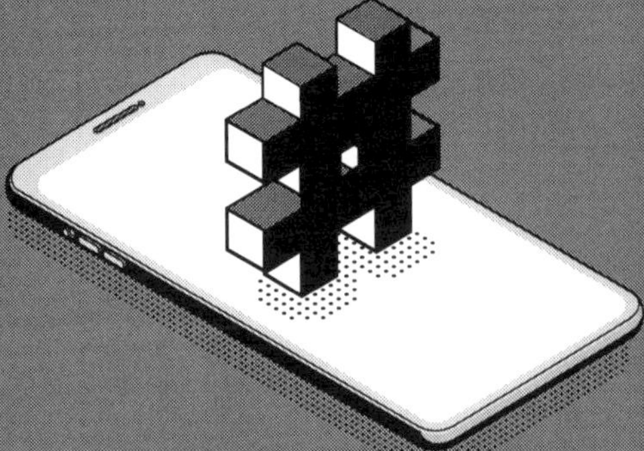

says she wants to be more present with me, to disconnect to connect. I learned from an article we both read that disconnecting from our smartphones from time to time helps us connect more with people around us.

And this is another digital decision: putting the smartphone in airplane mode or not taking the phone to the movies are decisions we make about our digital devices that will change our lives, whether we are near or far from them.

If you want to solve a difficult problem, focus on a task that requires more attention or connect with someone next to you, leave your phone in airplane mode, turn it off or keep it away from you.

EHITCS AND MORALS 2.0

ETHICS AND TECHNOLOGY IN THE FOURTH INDUSTRIAL REVOLUTION

Imagine a self-driving fully autonomous car coming at high speed. The car sees three pedestrians crossing the street. That's right; cars can see, they have computational vision, which is actually better than human vision for detecting obstacles and reading road signs. So, this car with three passengers drives at high speed and sees three people crossing the street in a crosswalk. The car needs to make a decision to either move forward or make a turn. The problem is that it has already identified a wall, and if it deviates, it will hit the wall and, due to the high speed, its three passengers will die. The car has two options:

1. Move on and kill three pedestrians.
2. Make a turn and kill three passengers.

What should it do? This is one of the digital decisions that robots will have to make for us, and who should decide what is right or wrong? The MIT created Moral Machine, a platform for collecting the human perspective on moral decisions made by intelligent machines such as autonomous cars. The examples get much more complex, as in the following images, where the car must decide between:

- Killing a doctor, a pregnant woman, two babies, and a dog; or
- Killing a pregnant woman, a dog, a homeless person, a girl and a boy.

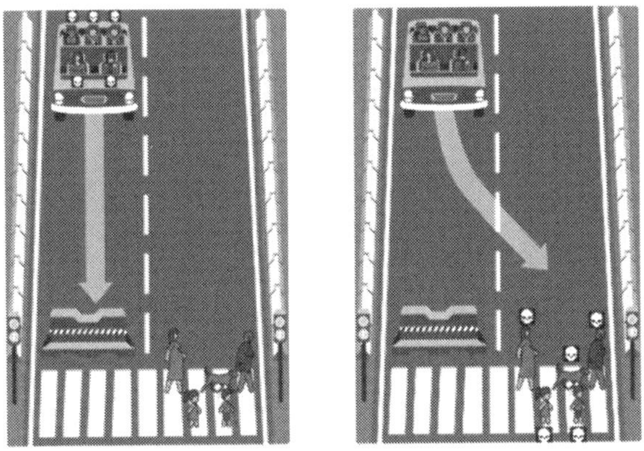

Just look at all the "boxes" into which people are categorized. Gender, profession, age... Should all these characteristics be taken into account at the time of such digital decision? If these are not the characteristics to consider, then which ones should be? What is right and wrong, what should and shouldn't be done is still being debated globally.

Should your autonomous car give more value to your life than a pedestrian's? And can your wearable activity be used against you in court? Should we allow drones to be the new paparazzi? Can human genes be patented?

The article "The Moral Dilemmas of the Fourth Industrial Revolution," published by the World Economic Forum, brought up many questions relevant to the moral and ethics of the digital age.

Scientists are already conflicted by these dilemmas. As we enter the new machine age, we need a new set of coded moral rules to become a global rule.

And this is starting to happen:

> In 2016, Carnegie Mellon University in the United States announced a new study center on the Ethics of Artificial Intelligence.
> During President Obama's administration, the White House published an article on the same subject.
> Technology giants like Facebook and Google have announced a partnership to build an ethical framework for AI.
> In 2018, Salesforce hired their first-ever Chief Ethical and Humane Use Officer

There are as many risks as there are opportunities: Stephen Hawking, Elon Musk, and other experts signed an open letter calling for efforts to be pooled to ensure that AI is beneficial to society.

The potential benefits are enormous, for all that civilization has to offer is the product of human intelligence; we cannot predict what we can achieve when this intelligence is enhanced by AI tools, but the eradication of disease and poverty is not unfathomable. Because of its great potential, it is important to research how to reap its benefits while avoiding any problems.[41]

These are big names and big ideals. Many efforts, however, have no global cooperation. Moreover, the implications of the Fourth Industrial Revolution go beyond the Internet and AI.

[41] The moral dilemmas of the Fourth Industrial Revolution. Available at: <https://www.weforum.org/agenda/2017/02/ethics-2-0-how-the-brave-new-world-needs-a-moral-compass/>. Accessed on: April, 2019.

Professor Klaus Schwab, founder of the World Economic Forum, believes that this phase will be built around "cyber-physical systems," in which the boundaries between the physical, the digital and the biological are attenuated. As we embrace the machine age, we will be faced with new ethical challenges, demanding new laws. In some cases, the whole moral code may need reworking. Such is the nature of technological advancements. I believe that humanity will soon be about to rethink ethics and morals 4.0.

The ethical implications range from the immediate (like the algorithms behind Facebook and Google that influence everything from our emotions to the elections) to the future (what happens if self-driving vehicles make the truck driver occupation disappear?).

The following is a sample of the ethical decisions we will face in four areas: Life sciences; Artificial Intelligence, machine learning, and data learning; social media and gadgets; robots and machines.

1. Life Sciences. Should gene editing be legal to manipulate the human race and create "designer babies"? Cancer researcher Siddhartha Mukherjee, in his critically acclaimed book *The Gene*, highlighted the deep ethical questions that advances in genome science will pose. The list of ethical questions is long: What if a pre-natal test predicted your child would have an IQ of 80 points, well below average, unless you undertook a little editing? What if these technologies were limited to only wealthy people?
2. AI, machine learning, and data. Over time, Artificial Intelligence will help us make all kinds of decisions. But how do we ensure these algorithms are fairly designed? How do we iron

out biases from such systems, which will eventually be used to determine job promotions, college admissions, and even our choice for a life partner? Should the local police use facial recognition software? Should predictive policing based on algorithms be legal? What impact will this have on our privacy? Will cutting-edge technology in the hands of local law enforcement usher in the era of the surveillance state?

3. Social media and gadgets. What if our Kindles were embedded with facial recognition software and biometric sensors, so that the device could tell how every sentence influenced our heart rate and blood pressure?
4. Bots and machines. How do we decide what driverless cars can do? How do we determine what robots can decide? Will there be a need for the robot equivalent of a Bill of Rights? What about the rights of humans to marry robots and of robots to own property? Should a highly advanced cyborg be allowed to run for political office?

In the old days, free markets decided the fate of innovations, and eventually governments came in and intervened (Uber is banned in Japan, for example, but it is allowed in India). However, in this case, this approach could be disastrous.

We do not want governments to stop innovation: We are calling for a coherent global dialogue on ethics in the 21st century. Dialogue needs to go beyond academic journals and opinion articles, and should include government committees and international bodies such as the UN.

So far we have had a silos approach—from the worldwide ban on human cloning to partial restrictions on transgenic foods. Different regions have also taken different positions and were not able to organize a unified response: The European Union's approach to managing the social impact of new technologies is markedly different from that of the United States. China, on the other hand, has always had a far-reaching vision. Technology is like water—it will find open spaces. In an interconnected world, local decisions are effective only when made possible by international consensus.

A structured international forum will be needed to draw up a list of technologies that require governance, evaluate each of these technologies, and come up with a plan for its code of conduct. For example, an international government body could establish specific rules such as making mandatory the exposition of the logical scheme behind certain AI algorithms.

The world of science has some successful examples of international cooperation, such as the 1987 Montreal Protocol (on the ozone depletion issue), and the 1975 Asilomar Conference (to regulate DNA technologies).

I agree with the conclusions of the World Economic Forum that humanity will face questions that it has not yet needed to answer. And so, we need to start talking now.

If we do not prepare in advance, we will face several risks. We risk losing too much power to machines and changing the course of humanity without fully understanding the consequences, creating a great deal of inequality between the "tech rich," as well as a huge subclass. Anyone who has seen a single episode of the award-winning

Black Mirror series should be concerned about the dystopian future that may lie ahead—if we do not address the complex philosophical and legal issues now.

Traditionally, technological advancements outpace the political process: We have already lost because we have not formulated a moral guide for the internet and are still trying to reach it to this day. We cannot afford to be blinded to the next frontiers, whether in biotechnology or AI. Our future is increasingly in the hands of engineers and entrepreneurs who will not necessarily be held accountable.

Society can adapt to changes—from steam engines to iPhones and a significant increase in life expectancy. As Bill Gates states, "technology is amoral." It is up to us to decide its uses and limits.

This article was also published on Medianama as "Ethics 2.0 – How The Brave New World Needs A Moral Compass."[42]

[42] MEDIANAMA. Ethics 2.0 – How the brave new world needs a Moral Compass, 2017. Available at: <http://www.medianama.com/2017/01/223-ethics-2-0-brave-new-world-needs-moral-compass/>. Accessed on: October 10, 2019.

WHAT NOW?

You must be wondering: "What now? What should I do with everything I've learned in this book?," "How to apply this learning in my life?," "How to keep improving?," "How can I be more digitally conscious?"

The whole point of this book is to raise your digital consciousness about digital nudges and the hidden forces that influence your digital decisions. Once you know how irrational you are, your cognitive biases, your systematic errors, it is easier to prevent them from taking over our lives.

NEXT STEPS TO RAISE YOUR DIGITAL CONSCIOUSNESS

Here are some recommended simple steps:

1. ACCEPT THAT YOU ARE DIGITALLY IRRATIONAL.
2. OBSERVE YOUR DIGITAL BEHAVIOR.
3. TRY MAKING SMALL CHANGES.
4. TALK TO OTHER PEOPLE AND LEARN TOGETHER.
5. GO BACK TO STEP 2 AND DO IT ALL OVER AGAIN...

1. ACCEPT THAT WE ARE DIGITALLY IRRATIONAL

Behavioral economics has opened our eyes and scientifically proved that we are irrational. We live increasingly immersed in the digital world. We know that we have limited attention and that we make more short-term decisions as opposed to long-term ones. The present self is more important and more powerful than the future self. We do not consume all the content that is available to us because it's humanly impossible and we don't pay attention to everything we click on or like. Despite all this, we need to be aware and conscious of our digital decisions. We are digitally irrational! Accepting it is the first step.

2. OBSERVE YOUR DIGITAL BEHAVIOR

In order to understand your current digital behavior, answer the questions:

> What digital habits do I have?

____

____

____

____

____

____

> What digital devices and apps do I use daily?

____

____

____

> What are the digital decisions I make in the digital world and which ones do the digital world make for me?

> How long and how much of my attention do I invest in digital devices?

To get a better look at things, I use a very good application called Quality Time. It provides a summary of my day on my phone.

The issue is not just how much time you use your phone, but what you do during that time.

#DigitalNudge

THE ISSUE IS NOT JUST HOW MUCH TIME YOU USE YOUR PHONE, BUT WHAT YOU DO DURING THAT TIME.

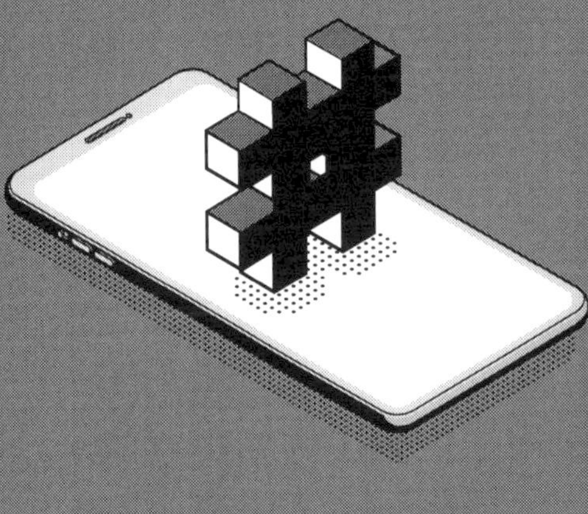

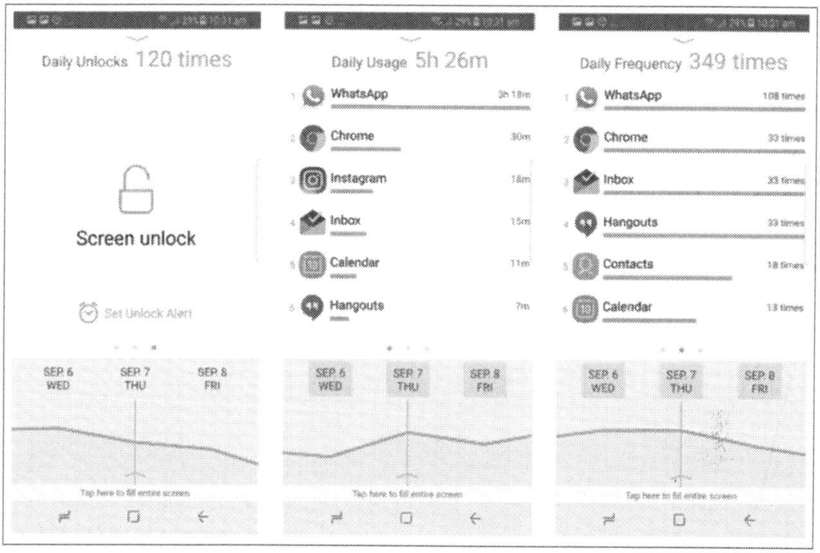

A few things I learned by observing my behavior through this app:

> WhatsApp is the app I use most on my smartphone.

> The number of times I unlock my phone screen has decreased over time.

> I spend an average of five hours a day on my smartphone.

These are all unquestionable facts and data. I can only observe and try to learn something about how I behave today.

More smartphone usage has never been a deathbed wish.

3. TRY TO MAKE SMALL CHANGES

After observing how you behave, think about what you want to change and what goals you want to achieve. Run small experiments with yourself, for example:

> Sleep with the smartphone outside the bedroom, away from you.

- Stop and think for two minutes at least five times a day before clicking on an online button.
- Go out without taking your smartphone with you once a week.

4. TALK TO OTHER PEOPLE AND LEARN TOGETHER.

Here we talk about Behavioral Economics issues, which apply to the 7 billion people in the world, and our digital irrationality issues, which apply to digital citizens—at least 4.3 billion people in the world. This number keeps growing. It's a lot of stuff and a lot of people to learn it, isn't it? So, spread the message. Learn with others.

5. GO BACK TO STEP 2 AND DO IT ALL OVER AGAIN...

We must always be open to experimenting with new habits and always pay close attention to our behavior. Remember that no change happens overnight, so repeat these steps and you will feel the positive transformation as you walk the path of raising your digital consciousness.

THIS IS JUST THE BEGINNING

This is a continuous process and not necessarily a linear one. This means starting by accepting, then observing, experimenting, and talking to others. It will very likely last for the rest of your life. Every day I learn something new, every day I run new experiments with myself and others, observe more about how I behave and keep learning from all the people with whom I relate in all dimensions of my life.

MORE SMARTPHONE USAGE HAS NEVER BEEN A DEATHBED WISH.

#DigitalNudge

The Fourth Industrial Revolution has begun: robots, Artificial Intelligence, machine learning, drones, refrigerators that order food on their own, cars that don't need drivers, computers that make medical diagnosis. All of those already exist and will increase in quantity and impact capacity exponentially.

After reading this book, it is very likely that you have raised your Digital Intelligence Quotient (QD) and leveled up in the Digital Consciousness Pyramid. I believe you are at least at level 2, and on your way to level 3! You have learned more and now have critical skills for your success, happiness, independence, and safety in the digital age.

The goal is an ongoing journey is to raise our awareness while making decisions that have a more positive impact to the world, decreasing manipulation and increasing the nudges for good. Since we will always be irrational, let's be more digitally conscious so that we build and live in a better world!

WHAT ARE PEOPLE SAYING ABOUT *DIGITAL NUDGE?*

Receiving praise, criticism or suggestions about a work helps the author improve the content. Many thanks to the following people, who have read this book and helped me make it broader so that you, the reader, enjoy reading it, as it should be!

I also want to hear what you think of the book! Please, contact me at: www.digitalnudge.org/book/qr/review and let's transform the digital world together!

"Reading it has taken me into the future and then brought me back to contemporary reality, aware that technology must become part of our lives, not its entirety. Fabio Pereira's research addressed in a practical and singular way the consumption of innovation in the world. All this with a graphic design that encourages the absorption of knowledge and makes reading more enjoyable and intuitive. It's a real handbook for those who don't want to be held hostage by technology."

Patrícia Basilio – economy and business journalist

"A light, pleasurable and intriguing read about what drives our decisions and how we can, in small details, change our lives and of those around us for the better! With a practical, realistic, and pragmatic view, Fabio shows us in his book, with facts, how we behave in our decisions, from the simplest to the most complex ones. Exploring the idea of nudges, one of the current hot topics around the world, the author discusses how little nudges in our daily lives can decisively transform behaviors. A key book for our age that addresses one of humanity's greatest challenges: How to change behaviors and habits for a better life and society!"

Flávia Ávila – CEO of InBehavior Lab, founder and editor of EconomiaComportamental.org and MBA coordinator at ESPM

"A must-read book when digital not only takes over the world, but also our minds."

Arthur Paredes – advertiser and author of *Profundamente*

"Fabio Pereira has insightfully identified and mapped the many existing cognitive biases and pitfalls in the online world. His book is a guide to the yellow brick road through which we become digitally conscious and avoid being hooked like fools while surfing online."

Anderson Mattozinhos – economist and founder of Geekonomics, has an MBA on Behavioral Economics

"In a world where habits and behaviors are highly digitized, Fabio Pereira bridges the gap between the physical and the virtual, helping us understand why we should be more conscious in our online and offline decision making."

Maria Augusta Ribeiro – specialist in Netnography and Digital Behavior

"In 2017 I was impacted by one of Fabio's talks on digital awareness. From then on, inspired by his words, I finally understood the subject. In his superb book, he subtly leads us to become, in fact, more digitally conscious."

Dani Guedes – startup advisor and creative advisor

"Through this book, Fabio introduces us to the complex reality of our relationship with technology—which is increasingly integrated into our daily routine and our lives—and the result of years of his multidisciplinary research. While reading the book, he guides us through complex themes of human behavior, relating human (ir)rationality in decision-making to technologies such as Artificial Intelligence and social media. In a very light, didactic, and at the same time impactful way, the author makes us think about digital awareness and how we can improve our experience in using technologies."

Wellington Lopes – Red Hat Academy

"It is impossible to read this digital behavior guide and continue acting the same way we used to. Fabio conveys in a very light way, but with scientific basis, relevant examples of how unawareness in the digital world can be dangerous. With his sensitive, inclusive, and humane eyes, he shows us positive alternatives for empowering ourselves while making digital decisions to ensure freedom of choice and autonomy. Everyone should read this book to stimulate a new awareness and to be less digitally influenced."

Georgia Lima – TEDx coordinator

"By merging simple concepts and information, but making complex considerations and assessments, Fabio is able to give a broad and in-depth insight into the behavioral relationships of the world within the digital and global ecosystem. The direct and objective approach makes us reflect on the imponderables that surround us about technology as well as its impacts on digital human relationships."

Roberto Hengist – head of Digital Innovation at Banco Votorantim

"Life in the digital age is a path of no return! So, the best option is to experience this world consciously, and the book *Digital Nudge* is perfect for that. A very light and dynamic reading, with lots of humor,

Fabio brings pertinent questions about our daily online behaviors and mainly about digital decisions that go beyond our choices and wishes. It's a very relevant book for the current time!"

Renata Albertim – co-founder of Mete a Colher

"In my view, this is a modern survival handbook. Simply and directly, Fabio show us the main tools being used online to help or harm us. Thus, he helps us become more aware and learn to make better decisions in networks and in everyday life."

Caio Ledesma – behavioral trainer

"As a practical, simple, and objective guide, *Digital Nudge* is a light reading that captivates us with so many discoveries. It is simply brilliant to approach a topic that seems so far away, but which is very present in every decision in our daily lives."

Felipe Lucena – teacher

"In a light and very interactive way, the book makes us reflect on all the acts in the digital world, broadening our awareness through the enormous knowledge Fabio has accumulated over the years, and the tips in this amazing book."

Hélica Pereira – CEO CrossPwr

"With simple vocabulary and everyday examples, Fabio will win the reader over with a fluid and intelligent reading. The book is a gift, with tips and insights on how to consciously navigate the digital world we are immersed in. I didn't know how unaware I was in the digital world until I read this book."

Andrea Pinto – project manager

"I really liked the text that explains about digital awareness connected to algorithmic biases when it comes to building software that impacts people's lives and can generate digital biases. The world needs more discussion about how technology is evolving and for whom."

Roselma Mendes – black feminist and intersectional developer

"The book *Digital Nudge* brought a new perspective to my mind, which is to think about the diversity and inclusion of data, not just about teams. The next challenge is to dialogue with people who program and organize the data in order to awaken them to diversity and inclusion. By doing so, we no longer perpetuate skewed and biased analyzes."

Lisiane Lemos – technology specialist and Forbes Under 30

"The content of the book is amazing, very interesting, and shows us the unknown side of a seemingly well-known world: the digital one. I am really overwhelmed by how other people make decisions for us every day. The book, in fact, achieves its intended purpose: to change the reader! After reading, surely all readers will be much more aware of all their digital interactions. It is impossible to read this book and keep the same behavior and thinking. I have already started my change and my experiments."

Luciana Silva – agile coach

"With a very pleasant reading, Fabio seems to be talking to the reader... This book made me reflect on how the 'world' ceased to be the 'planet'. *Digital Nudge* supposes a journey without borders, making knowledge available a tool."

Fabíola Vieira – technical analyst at Sebrae

"A nudge sometimes is what we need to make a good decision and save lives. A push—small, timely and easy—to live in a better society. This is the case for Austria, where people are organ donors unless they check the opt-out option. Fabio's book looks at the psychological behaviors that influence decision making in the digital world, which is inevitably immersed in the physical world. With a clear language and relevant examples, he explains behavioral science from the perspective of the digital world: the digital awareness."

Paulo Caroli – author of *Lean Inception* and consultant

"Using a straightforward language and extreme clarity, Fabio Pereira captures the zeitgeist of this virtual age by lucidly discussing digital choices, decisions, and nudges, leading the reader through a joyful journey of cyber discoveries. The reader is led into a pleasurable and timely state of self-awareness that will make them safer from the endless and vast ocean of the internet."

Paulo Neto – journalist and film and theater critic

"With a dynamic reading, this book can bring reader and author closer in a light, fun, and interesting conversation. Understanding that our digital decisions go beyond what we consciously realize may be revealing at first, but above all it is liberating! It makes us more critical technology users, while also showing us the wonderful evolution of human relationships with technology. I found the reading addictive. Each topic was so interesting that it made me want to read through and understand what conclusion I could draw."

Renata Lourena – software developer and consultant

"*Digital Nudge* brings about a series of questions about how we are facing the digital age and decisions that are often not consciously made by us. Fabio has written a very relevant book that stimulates reflection, addressing real life examples and, above all, tips on how we can pay more attention and whether we are being influenced or not in the digital environment."

Scheila Giongo – project manager

"The book presents a delightful and useful reading about the power of the digital age on human behavior. It is an excellent source of reflection and change. With simple, clear, and grounded language, Fabio leads us to reflect on how much the digital world interferes with our awareness and, ultimately, with our decisions."

Teresa M. M. Maciel – UFPE's CTO

REFERENCES

ARIELY, Dan. *Previsivelmente irracional*: Como as situações do dia a dia influenciam nossas decisões?. 4th ed. Rio de Janeiro: Elsevier, 2008. 256 p.

BENARTZI, Shlomo; LEHRER, Jonah. *The Smarter Screen*: Surprising Ways to Influence and Improve Online Behavior. New York: Portfolio, 2015.

BULLYING STATISTICS. *Cyber Bullying Statistics*. Available at: <www.bullyingstatistics.org/content/cyber-bullying-statistics.html>. Accessed on: May 9, 2019.

CANAL TECH. *O que é e como usar o Duolingo*. Available at: <www.canaltech.com.br/internet/O-que-e-e-como-usar-o-Duolingo>. Accessed on: May 9, 2019.

CIRILLO, Francesco. *The Pomodoro Technique*: The Acclaimed Time-Management System that Has Transformed How We Work. New York: Currency, 2018.

CONSTINE, John. Google Reportedly Offered $30 billion to Acquire Snapchat. *Tech Crunch*, August 3, 2017. Available at: <www.techcrunch.com/2017/08/03/google-buy-snap>. Accessed on: May 9, 2019.

______________. Why Is Facebook Page Reach Decreasing? More Competition and Limited Attention. *Tech Crunch*, April 3, 2017. Available at: <www.techcrunch.com/2014/04/03/the-filtered-feed-problem>. Accessed on: May 9,2019.

CULTURA ÁGIL. *Kanban*: do início ao fim!. Available at: <https://www.culturaagil.com.br/kanban-do-inicio-ao-fim/>. Accessed on: May 9, 2019.

CUNHA, Carolina. "Tecnologia – O que é a 4ª revolução industrial?" *UOL*. Available at: <https://vestibular.uol.com.br/resumo-das-disciplinas/atualidades/tecnologia-o-que-e-a-4-revolucao-industrial.htm>. Accessed on: May 9, 2019.

CZERWONKA, Mariana. "Sono e cansaço representam 60% dos acidentes no país". *Porta do Trânsito*, April 16, 2013. Disponivel em: <www.portaldotransito.com.br/noticias/sono-e-cansaco-representam-60-dos-acidentes-no-pais-2>. Accessed on: May 9, 2019.

DARKPATTERNS. *What Are Dark Patterns?*. Available at: <www.darkpatterns.org>. Accessed on: May 9, 2019.

DEMARTINI, Marina. "Um breve histórico da briga entre Facebook e Snapchat". *Exame*, August 3, 2016. Available at: <www.exame.abril.com.br/tecnologia/um-breve-historico-da-briga-entre-facebook-e-snapchat>. Accessed on: May 9, 2019.

DMR BUSINESS STATISTICS. 95 *Amazing Android Statistics and Facts* (2019) – By the number. Available at: <www.expandedramblings.com/index.php/android-statistics>. Accessed on: May 9, 2019.

DQ INSTITUTE. Available at: <www.dqinstitute.org>. Accessed on: May 9, 2019.

DUOLINGO. *What Is A Streak?*. Available at: <www.support.duolingo.com/hc/en-us/articles/204980880-What-is-a-streak->. Accessed on: May 9, 2019.

__________. *Why You Should Keep Up A Streak*. Available at: <www.duolingo.

com/comment/5865479/Why-you-should-keep-up-a-streak>. Accessed on: May 9, 2019.

ECONOMIA COMPORTAMENTAL. *Econs e Humanos (Econs and Humans)*. Available at: <www.economiacomportamental.org/econs-e-humanos-econs-and-humans>. Accessed on: May 9, 2019.

______________________________. *Guia de Economia Comportamental e Experimental*. Available at: <www.economiacomportamental.org/guia>. Accessed on: May 9, 2019.

ESTRATEGISTAS. *A ascensão da economia da atenção, por Isaac Lewis*. Available at: <www.estrategistas.com/ascensao-economia-da-atencao>. Accessed on: May 9, 2019.

EYAL, Nir; HOOVER, Ryan. *Hooked: How to Build Habit-Forming Products*. New York: Portfolio, 2014.

FOUNDATION TEAM. *37 Mind Blowing YouTube Statistics For B2B Marketers In 2019*. Available at: <https://foundationinc.co/lab/youtube-statistics-b2b-marketers/>. Accessed on: May 17, 2019.

FUZARO, Nathalia. "Joy of missing out: entenda o que é JOMO, a alegria de não estar em todas". *Glamour*, March 24, 2018. Available at: <www.revistaglamour.globo.com/Lifestyle/Must-Share/noticia/2018/03/joy-missing-out-entenda-o-que-e-jomo-alegria-de-nao-estar-em-todas.html>. Accessed on: May 9, 2019.

GARDNER, Howard. *Estruturas da mente*: a teoria das inteligências múltiplas. 2nd ed. Porto Alegre: Editora Penso, 1994.

GIANTOMASO, Isabela. "O que é FoMO? 'Fear of missing out' revela o medo de ficar por fora nas redes sociais". *Tech Tudo*, May 27, 2017. Available at: <www.techtudo.com.br/noticias/2017/05/o-que-e-fomo

-fear-of-missing-out-revela-o-medo-deficar-por-fora-nas-redes-sociais.ghtml>. Accessed on: May 9, 2019.

INSTITUTO HUMANITAS UNISINOS. "Os dilemas morais da Quarta Revolução Industrial". Available at: <www.ihu.unisinos.br/571796-os-dilemasmorais-da-quarta-revolucao-industrial>. Accessed on: May 9, 2019.

KAHNEMAN, Daniel; LEITE, Cássio De Arantes. *Rápido e devagar*: Duas formas de pensar. Rio de Janeiro: Objetiva, 2012.

LEE, Dave. "Facebook considera ter botão de 'não curtir', diz Zuckerberg". G1, December 12, 2014. Available at: <www.g1.globo.com/tecnologia/noticia/2014/12/facebook-considera-ter-botao-de-nao-curtir-diz-zuckerberg.html>. Accessed on: May 9,2019.

LINKEDIN. "Escritor de 'Nudge' ganha Nobel". Available at: <www.linkedin.com/pulse/escritor-de-nudge-ganha-nobel-fabio-pereira>. Accessed on: May 9, 2019.

LOMAS, Natasha. "Amazon Patents 'Anticipatory' Shipping – To Start Sending Stuff Before You've Bought It". Available at: <https://techcrunch.com/2014/01/18/amazon-pre-ships/>. Accessed on: May 9, 2019

LOPES, Maria Graciete Carramate. "Vírus – Estrutura e ciclos virais". UOL Educação. Available at: <https://educacao.uol.com.br/disciplinas/biologia/virus-estrutura-e-ciclos-virais.htm?cmpid=copiaecola>. Accessed on: May 15,2019.

MARTINELLI, Andrea. "A polêmica sobre paternidade e estereótipos que o vídeo das crianças 'invadindo' entrevista ao vivo gerou". *Huffington Post Brasil*, March 11, 2017. Available at: <www.

huffpostbrasil.com/2017/03/11/a-polemica-sobre-paternidade-e-estereotipos-que-o-video-das-cria_a_21879949>. Accessed on: May 9,2019.

MCKINSEY, Global Institute. "O futuro do mercado de trabalho: impacto em empregos, habilidades e salários". Available at: <https://www.mckinsey.com/featured-insights/future-of-work/jobs-lost-jobs-gained-what-the-future-of-work-will-mean-for-jobs-skills-and-wages/pt-br>. Accessed on: June 11, 2019.

MINDSET DIGITAL. "The Power of Streaks". Available at: <www.mindsetdigital.com/snapchat-streaks-gamification/>. Accessed on: May 9, 2019.

MORAL MACHINE. MIT, *Máquina moral*. Available at: <www.moralmachine.mit.edu/hl/pt>. Accessed on: May 9, 2019.

MUKHERJEE, Siddhartha. *O gene*: Uma história íntima. São Paulo: Companhia das Letras, 2016.

MULLER, Nicolas. "O que é o Snapchat e como usar?". *Oficina da Net*, January 6, 2016. Available at: <www.oficinadanet.com.br/post/15802-o-que-e-o-snapchat-e-como-usar>. Accessed on: May 9, 2019.

NA PRÁTICA. "Técnica Pomodoro: aprenda a gerenciar seu tempo para executar mais". Available at: <www.napratica.org.br/pomodoro>. Accessed on: May 9, 2019.

NIR & FAR. "Technology is Distracting and Addictive. Here's How to Fix It". Available at: <www.nirandfar.com/2017/04/deal-persuasive-technology-video.html>. Accessed on: May 9, 2019.

NPJ LEARN COMMUNITY. "Cognitive Costs of the Mere Presence of Smartphones". Available at: <www.npjscilearncommunity.nature.

com/users/60608-kristen-duke/posts/19475-cognitive-costs-of-the-mere-presence-of-smartphones>. Accessed on: May 9, 2019.

NVIDIA. "What's The Difference Between Deep Learning Training and Inference?" Available at: <www.blogs.nvidia.com/blog/2016/08/22/difference-deep-learning-training-inference-ai>. Accessed on: May 9, 2019.

RIBEIRO, Gabriel Francisco. "Você vai falar com os eletrônicos da sua casa, e quem vai responder é Alexa". UOL, January 9, 2017. Available at: <www.noticias.uol.com.br/tecnologia/noticias/redacao/2017/01/09/voce-sabe-o-que-e-alexa-assistente-pessoal-pode-invadir-sua-vida-em-breve.htm>. Accessed on: May 9, 2019.

QUIN TECH. Available at: <https://quintech.io/>. Accessed on: May 15, 2019.

REUTERS. "New Zealand Passport Robot Tells Applicant of Asian Descent to Open Eyes". Available at: <www.reuters.com/article/us-newzealand-passport-error/new-zealand-passport-robot-tells-applicant-of-asian-descent-to-open-eyes-idUSKBN13W0RL>. Accessed on: May 9, 2019.

RODRIGUES, Yann. "A maior lista de vieses cognitivos que você já viu (provavelmente)". *Medium*, April 26, 2017. Available at: <https://www.medium.com/al%C3%A9m-do-roteiro/a-maior-lista-de-vieses-cognitivos-que-voc%C3%AA-j%C3%A1-viu-provavelmente-3b57e1350be5>. Accessed on: October 12, 2019.

SCARCITY. "Behavioral Economics". Available at: <https://www.behavioraleconomics.com/resources/mini-encyclopedia-of-be/scarcity-heuristic/>. Accessed on: October 1, 2019.

SCARCITY Bias. "Tutor 2 U". Available at: <https://www.tutor2u.net/economics/reference/behavioural-economics-scarcity-bias>. Accessed on: October 12, 2019.

SCHWAB, Klaus. *A Quarta Revolução Industrial*. São Paulo: Edipro, 2016.

SHAMSIAN, Jacob. "Teens Are Obsessed with This One Snapchat Score that Can Make or Break Friendships". *Business Insider,* December 15, 2016.Available at: <www.businessinsider.com/teens-are-obsessed-with-snap-streaks-on-snapchat-2016-12>. Accessed on: May 9, 2019.

SMART CAP. Available at: <www.smartcaptech.com>. Accessed on: February, 2018.

SNAPCHAT. Support Snapchat. Available at: <www.support.snapchat.com/pt-BR/a/Snaps-snapstreak>. Accessed on: May 9, 2019.

STANFORD UNIVERSITY. VHIL – Virtual Human Interaction Lab. Available at: <https://vhil.stanford.edu/>. Accessed on: May 9, 2019.

SULLER, John. "The Online Disinhibition Effect". Available at: <www.liebertpub.com/doi/abs/10.1089/1094931041291295>. Accessed on: April,2019.

PRADO, Jean. "Bem-estar digital: o que é e como ativar no Android 9 Pie". *Tecnoblog*. Available at: <www.tecnoblog.net/260237/bem-estar-digital-android-pie>. Accessed on: May 9, 2019.

TED. *How I'm Fighting Bias in Algorithms*. Available at: <www.ted.com/talks/joy_buolamwini_how_i_m_fighting_bias_in_algorithms>. Accessed on: May 9,2019.

_____. *The Jobs We'll Lose to Machines – And The Ones We Won't*. Available at: <www.ted.com/talks/anthony_goldbloom_the_jobs_we_ll_lose_to_machines_and_the_ones_we_won_t>. Accessed on: May 9,2019.

THALER, Richard H.; SUNSTEIN, Cass R. *Nudge*: Improving Decisions About Health, Wealth, and Happiness. 1st ed. Estados Unidos: Penguin, 2009.

______________________. *Nudge*: O empurrão para a escolha certa. São Paulo: Elsevier, 2009.

THE MEDICAL FUTURIST. "5 Ways Medical Virtual Reality Is Already Changing Healthcare". Available at: <www.medicalfuturist.com/5-ways-medical-vr-is-changing-healthcare>. Accessed on: May 9, 2019.

TOLLE, Eckhart. *The Power of Now*: A Guide to Spiritual Enlightenment. Novato: New World Library, 2010.

UNCTV SCIENCE. "How Many Daily Decisions Do We Make?". Available at: <http://science.unctv.org/content/reportersblog/choices>.Accessed on: May 15, 2019.

UOL ECONOMIA. "Facebook registra lucro líquido de US$ 15,9 bilhões em 2017, alta de 56%". Available at: <www.economia.uol.com.br/noticias/efe/2018/01/31/facebook-registra-lucro-liquido-de-us-159-bilhoes-em-2017-alta-de-56.htm>. Accessed on: May 9, 2019.

SEWARD JR., Kennedy. "How Virtual Reality Can Be Used to Fight Racism and Prejudice in Society". *Upload*, April 29, 2017. Available at: <www.uploadvr.com/vr-fight-racism-prejudice>. Accessed on: May 9, 2019.

WANSINK, Brian; SOBAL, Jeffrey. *Mindless eating*: the 200 daily food decisions we overlook, Environment and Behavior. New York: Bantam Books, 2007.

WASHINGTON POST. Transcript of Mark Zuckerberg's Senate hearing. Available at: <www.washingtonpost.com/news/the-switch/wp/2018/

04/10/transcript-of-mark-zuckerbergs-senate-hearing/?utm_term=.9c4720b85f61>. Accessed on: May 9, 2019.

WIKIPEDIA. List of Cognitive Biases. Available at: <https://en.wikipedia.org/wiki/List_of_cognitive_biases>. Accessed on: October 12, 2019.

If you prefer a digital version, scan the QR code to acess all the references.

ABOUT EDITORA CAROLI

For readers and authors who seek and share knowledge quickly, Editora Caroli is a small publisher—all books are written, read, edited and/or revised by Paulo Caroli, who assists in the production, dissemination and distribution of books and e-books. Unlike traditional publishing houses, Editora Caroli gives access to knowledge in its essence, offering new content via free e-books, as well as supporting events and educational entities, presenting them with free books and e-books.

At www.caroli.org you will find this and other quality content. Enjoy our free materials!

WIP (WRITING IN PROGRESS)

Editora Caroli presents a new work proposal, bringing authors closer to their readers from the beginning of content production. Why wait for the author to finish writing to find out if the content is any good? In today's world this no longer makes sense. For this reason, Editora Caroli promotes sharing (for free whenever possible) of WIP through e-book formats (.pdf, .mobi and .epub). This way, readers have quick access to new ideas and can be part of the development of the work. For the authors, it is an effective form of feedback and motivation for content creation.

FABIO PEREIRA is a TEDx speaker and coach, a futurist technologist focused on people and behavior. His innovative and provoking ideas about the brain science behind the digital world have led him to speak at several conferences and events in Australia, United States, Brazil, China and Germany.

Fabio is the Head of Open Innovation Labs Latin America at Red Hat. He has 19 years of experience, 10 of those at ThoughtWorks Australia where he acted as Digital Transformation Advisor for clients including the Australian Government Digital Transformation Agency.

With a dream of becoming a billionaire, but not financially, he wishes to positively impact the lives of a billion people, a billion digital citizens. Fabio is passionate about human behaviour and believes that understanding the hidden forces that drive the 35,000 decisions we make every day can change our lives for good.

Follow the author at:
www.fabiopereira.me
fabiopereirame
fabiopereira.me
fabiopereirame
fabipereirame

Printed in Great Britain
by Amazon

44723506R00111